Evangelism & Discipleship

IN AFRICAN-AMERICAN CHURCHES

Books from the Institute for Black Family Development

The Black Family: Past, Present, and Future
(Lee N. June and Matthew Parker, editors)

Evangelism and Discipleship in African-American Churches
(Lee N. June and Matthew Parker, editors)

Men to Men: Perspectives of Sixteen African-American Christian Men (Lee N. June and Matthew Parker, editors)

Women to Women: Perspectives of Fifteen African-American Christian Women (Norvella Carter and Matthew Parker, editors)

LEE N. JUNE PH.D. - EDITOR
MATTHEW PARKER - CONSULTING EDITOR

Evangelism & Discipleship

IN AFRICAN-AMERICAN CHURCHES

ZondervanPublishingHouse
Grand Rapids, Michigan

A Division of HarperCollinsPublishers

Evangelism and Discipleship in African-American Churches
Copyright © 1999 by the Institute for Black Family Development

Requests for information should be addressed to:

🏛 ZondervanPublishingHouse
Grand Rapids, Michigan 49530

Library of Congress Cataloging-in-Publication Data

Evangelism and discipleship in African-American churches / Lee N. June, editor ;
   Matthew Parker, consulting editor.
        p.   cm.
    Includes bibliographical references.
    ISBN 0-310-22139-0 (softcover)
    1. Afro-American churches. 2. Church renewal—United States. I. June, Lee N. II.
Parker, Matthew, 1945–.
   BR563.N4E95 1999
   277.3'0089'96073—dc21   98-51522
                                                             CIP

Interior design by Sherri L. Hoffman

Printed in the United States of America

---

99 00 01 02 03 04 05 06 /❖ DC/ 10 9 8 7 6 5 4 3 2 1

Contents

97981

Preface

Historically, African-American churches have been the preeminent institution in the African-American community for strengthening, sustaining, and stabilizing families. Since their formal inception in America in the eighteenth century, African-American churches have performed vital spiritual, cultural, social, economic, educational, health, social welfare, and community and leadership development functions. In addition to forming educational facilities at all levels, Black religious institutions have been instrumental in creating life insurance companies, banks, credit unions, hospitals, nursing homes, funeral homes, orphanages, and housing for the elderly and low income families. They have provided food, clothing, and shelter to the needy. Beneficiaries of these efforts have included many community residents who are not church members.

There are many in our churches, like the people in this book, whom God has given a burden and gift for evangelism and discipleship. Because the Great Commission says, "Go and make disciples of all nations, baptizing them in the name of the Father and of the Son and of the Holy Spirit, and teaching them to obey everything I have commanded you" (Matthew 28:19–20), the local body of believers must be the source of evangelism and discipleship.

This book features individuals from African-American churches who are on the front line of evangelism and discipleship, who are leading with imaginative and innovative ways, and who have a desire to see more effective evangelism and discipleship in our churches and communities. My expectation is that this book will be used to increase one's personal skill level and/or to train others so that they may effectively and systematically evangelize and disciple people of all ages. The strength of our communities in the twenty-first century depends on it.

MATTHEW PARKER, PRESIDENT
INSTITUTE FOR BLACK FAMILY DEVELOPMENT, DETROIT

This book represents the third project Matthew Parker, president of the Institute for Black Family Development, and I have collaborated on under the auspices of the Institute. The first book was *The Black Family: Past, Present and Future* (Zondervan, 1991), in which Christian men and women shared their expertise on critical issues facing the family. In the second project, *Men to Men* (Zondervan, 1996), African-American men offered practical suggestions and solutions for issues facing our communities. In recognition of the fact that women were also facing such issues, the book was released in concert with *Women to Women* (Norvella Carter and Matthew Parker, Zondervan, 1996). It is our hope that these books are helping the body of Christ grow strong as it faces various challenges and opportunities.

With this book, the tradition of providing materials for helping men and women grow in maturity and effectiveness continues. The current focus is on evangelism and discipleship—the twin keys for reaching and developing men and women in the faith. African-American and other churches are relatively rich in membership (though evangelism is still much needed) but have been lax in discipling those in our midst. Therefore, we have assembled a group of diverse writers who can speak to these twins and offer insights and practical how-to's.

We are challenged to continue to work to fulfill the Great Commission in the twenty-first century. It is our hope that a more systematic connection will be made between evangelism (winning souls) and discipling (developing those who have been won) in the years ahead. This book is intended to assist in making this connection more feasible.

This book is divided into five parts. Part 1 deals with history and features two prominent African-Americans—V. Simpson Turner, who shows in dramatic form how we as a people have been involved in evangelism from the "rebirth" of this nation as America, and the late Tom Skinner, a twentieth-century pioneer who appeared on the evangelistic scene during the 1960s and was an important voice of reason and hope for college students who were dealing with identity issues in a nation at war with itself. Skinner shares a vivid analysis of where we have been and where we need to go to make evangelism effective. Both of these chapters are adaptations of their original presentations made at Atlanta 1988, a historical conference on evangelism.

In part 2, three writers address the role of the church and its primary officers. Willie Richardson, a well-known and respected pastor, covers what churches can and must do. Lloyd Blue, a former pastor who is now involved in training pastors and conducting church growth and development seminars, discusses how vital the pastor's role is and what the pastor can do to be maximally effective. Lee June presents the challenges for deacons.

Part 3 features Roland Hardy and David Gough. These chapters focus on Christian education and youth ministry. They argue for effective Christian education departments and the effective use of music in reaching youth.

Part 4 shows how individuals and groups can and must be involved. Michael Lyles deals with fatherhood and portrays this role as the "ultimate head coaching job." Norvella Carter shares her insights on the issues and opportunities for wives and mothers while Christopher Mathis focuses on youth and college students (two extremely fertile but often neglected areas of evangelism and discipleship).

Finally, part 5 covers missionaries and professionals. Joseph Jeter, a pioneering missionary, challenges the church to make greater use of missionaries and presents how missionaries can be maximally effective in working with the African-American church community. The final chapter by Hank Allen is intended to challenge the growing cadre of professionals to recognize their privileged responsibilities and utilize their opportunities.

Thanks is extended to all of the writers for allowing me to assemble their expertise and wisdom into one volume. I have been personally enriched by the experience. Mr. Matthew Parker, as consulting editor, is to be commended for his vision and unselfish dedication. His counsel has been invaluable. A special thanks to Ms. Anna Yokoyama for her assistance in typing the manuscript and for contacting contributors as necessary. Without her, the project would have been much delayed.

Finally, I offer this book to you in hopes that God will be glorified and that we will all develop into mature persons—persons who have been evangelized and are being biblically discipled.

LEE N. JUNE, PH.D.
EDITOR
EAST LANSING, MICHIGAN

PART ONE

History of African-American Evangelism

V. SIMPSON TURNER SR.

A History of African-American Evangelistic Activity

V. SIMPSON TURNER SR. is the pastor of Mt. Carmel Baptist Church in Brooklyn, New York, where he has served for the last thirty-four years. He earned a bachelor's degree from Gordon College in Wenham, Massachusetts; a master of religious education degree from the Biblical Seminary of New York City; a master of sacred theology degree from New York Theological Seminary; and a doctor of ministry degree from Drew University in Madison, New Jersey. He has served on many boards and has taught at several seminaries. He produced and directed a weekly radio show, *The Black Religious Experience,* for ten years.

Turner is the author of the book *Compassion for the City* and for ten years was the editor of *Baptist Progress,* the official journal of the Progressive National Baptist Convention. He is married to Laura B. Turner, and they have two children: V. Simpson Turner Jr. and Vivian Renee Pittman.

CHAPTER 1

V. SIMPSON TURNER SR.

A History of African-American Evangelistic Activity

INTRODUCTION*

Where did evangelism among African-Americans begin? The European slave trade began in 1444, continued for more than four hundred years, and resulted in the loss of forty million Africans from the African continent. During this period, 20 million Africans were brought to the New World as slaves, while millions more died in Africa during and after their capture or on ships or plantations (Bennett 1964). Descendants of the first slaves, Black Christians born in Spain and Portugal, were among the first settlers of the New World. Black explorers, servants, and slaves accompanied French families and Portuguese explorers in expeditions to North and South America (Bennett 1964). Twenty Blacks landed at Jamestown, Virginia, aboard a Dutch ship in 1619, and involuntary servitude, or slavery, of Africans in the New World had began.

BLACK EVANGELISM IN THE SEVENTEENTH CENTURY

The majority of Blacks came to America as slaves. Blacks were slaves in the thirteen colonies 113 years before the birth of George Washington and in the New World 244 years before the signing of the Emancipation Proclamation, according to historian Lerone Bennett (1964).

A typical slave trader was a pious captain such as John Newton, who prior to his conversion held prayer services twice a day on the slave ship and later wrote the famous hymns "Amazing Grace" and "How Sweet the Name of Jesus Sounds" (Bennett 1964). Every attempt was made to demean Africans and cause them to develop a slave mentality. For

---

*This chapter is based on a presentation given at Atlanta 1988 (Congress on Evangelizing Black America).

17

example, families were separated, and they were not permitted to use their native language or practice their native religions. Men were whipped into unconsciousness and slashed with knives. Women, too, were whipped, some while obviously pregnant. Due to the continuing slave trade and births, the slave population was ever increasing. There were 50,000 slaves in the colonies in 1710, and by 1776, when the Declaration of Independence was signed, the number had jumped to 500,000.

At first slave traders and slave owners rationalized the use of Africans as slaves because the Africans were not Christians,* but some slaveholders who were Christian preachers began to evangelize their slaves. Thus, with slaves becoming Christians, the rationale for slavery shifted to race during the period of 1667 through 1682 by the passage of new laws.

While most Blacks saw very little value in the White version of Christianity, some did respond and came into the Christian church. Through this evangelizing of slaves, God found a way to get the gospel of Jesus Christ to the greater slave population. He used illiterate slaves as preachers and exhorters to proclaim the gospel to slaves and slaveholders alike. They told slaveholders that God said to "let My people go." They told fellow slaves that God was not unaware of their oppression but that one day He would set His people free. They recited the story of the Hebrews in bondage and of God's sending Moses to tell Pharaoh to let His people go. They told how God followed up His message with plagues until Pharaoh agreed to let the Hebrews go. The preachers prophesied that this same God would in like manner rescue His chosen Black Israel if they would believe in Him.

These illiterate exhorters were taught to read by some sympathetic Whites and Black freedmen. As soon as Blacks in both the North and South were able to read the Bible and other literature, they became greatly influenced by the Pietist movement, which had been founded by Lutheran Philip Spener (1635–1705) in Germany and had spread to America. Slave preachers dedicated themselves to Bible reading and proclaimed the gospel of personal faith in Christ as well as social salvation from the bondage of economic, social, and political servitude. They also

---

*However, there is growing evidence that suggests that some of these people had already been exposed to Christianity while on African shores. Further, based on the listings of peoples in Acts 2:1–11, Blacks heard the gospel on the Day of Pentecost.

pointed out that Christians should be able to record their conversion experiences. That is why to this day in our churches people stand up and testify of the time they found the Lord and were converted.

The simple gospel of faith and the gift of God's grace was attractive to Blacks. The worship services were filled with enthusiastic singing and emotional responses. James Stallings, in his book *Telling the Story: Evangelism in Black Churches* (1988), says that Blacks took this European-American White Christianity, baptized it in African traditional culture, and created a new African-American Christianity.

BLACK EVANGELISM IN THE EIGHTEENTH CENTURY

Leadership in the evangelical movement in the late 1700s was multi-racial. For instance, Francis Asbury, a White Methodist bishop, was led by God to have as his traveling companion on his itinerant preaching mission an illiterate Black preacher named Harry Hosier. Hosier had more convicting power than the bishop and was marvelously used by God to lead the unconverted to Christ.

Drugs, alcohol, and depravity were just as relevant to the evangelistic messengers of the late 1700s as they are today. The story is told of John Stewart, a mulatto, who was a drug and alcohol addict. There were no drug treatment centers in those days, but John Stewart wandered into a Methodist revival meeting one night just in time to hear the sermon. By the time the sermon ended, John was under conviction. He found his way to the mourners bench, and there God dealt with him. He cried out to the Lord, and the Lord heard him and delivered him on the spot from his drug and alcohol addiction and whatever else held him in bondage. (For additional information on Stewart's life, see Woodson 1921, pp. 58–61.)

Doors were open and provisions were made for Stewart to receive training in Bible and missions. He felt led by God to go to Ohio to minister to the Wyandot Indians as a missionary evangelist. God used him mightily in that work. Stewart is credited with initiating home missions in the Methodist church. If God would touch some of us today to go evangelizing around our nation and win souls for Him, what a better nation and what better communities we would have.

From the time of the great spiritual awakenings of the eighteenth century, Blacks began separating from integrated revival meetings at which both Blacks and Whites preached to mixed congregations. Blacks, on the one hand, felt more comfortable and freer listening to their own preachers. Whites, on the other hand, often referred to Blacks as nuisances because of their emotional outbursts at worship, communion, and prayer services. The natural flow was the establishment of Black independent churches and denominations. In 1773 George Liele and Andrew Bryan, both former slaves with modest education and both preaching without compensation, organized the first Negro Baptist Church in the American colonies at Savannah, Georgia.

Later, in 1787, a quasi-religious organization called the Free African Society, was founded in Philadelphia when Richard Allen and Absalom Jones grew tired of being ordered to move to a reserved worship area for Blacks in the balcony of St. Georgia's Methodist Church. The Free African Society's services included a fund for mutual aid, burial aid, and relief for widows and orphans; programs for strengthening marriages and personal morality; cooperation with abolitionist societies; and correspondence with free Blacks.

Theological differences prompted Jones and Allen to go in different directions. Being attracted by Anglicanism, Absalom Jones became the rector of the first separate Protestant Episcopal Congregation for Blacks. On June 10, 1794, Richard Allen founded the Bethel African Methodist Episcopal (AME) Church (the first AME church in America). Later, on April 9, 1816, the AME Church, the first all-Black religious denomination in the United States, was formally organized in Philadelphia. Richard Allen was named the first bishop of the church, and upon Allen's death in 1831, Morris Brown, an exile from South Carolina, then residing in Philadelphia, became the head of the AME denomination.

Newport Gardner, an ex-slave, taught himself to read, sing, and write music. He was one of the first Black music teachers in America. He was also a preacher and founder of the Newport, Massachusetts, Colored Union Church in 1791. He became a missionary to Africa in 1826 and died there. James Varick, among others, organized the AME Zion denomination in 1821, and he became its first bishop.

And so on went the founding of new Black institutions until not only were these churches interested in saving souls at home, but also in saving souls abroad, particularly those on the mother continent of Africa. They used as biblical mandates Psalm 68:31: "Envoys will come from Egypt; Cush will submit herself to God"; and Acts 16:9–10: "During the night Paul had a vision of a man of Macedonia standing and begging him, 'Come over to Macedonia and help us.' After Paul had seen the vision, we got ready at once to leave for Macedonia, concluding that God had called us to preach the gospel to them."

Black independent churches heeded what they referred to as the Macedonian call to go to Africa, Haiti, and the Caribbean to plant churches. David George was the first Black Baptist missionary to go to Sierra Leone. George Liele, one of the founders of the first Black Baptist church, whom I mentioned earlier, became a missionary and went to Kingston, Jamaica. By 1793 there were five hundred converts in Jamaica, and Liele began an evangelical movement of Jamaican Baptists. From Jamaica, Liele sent out forty workers to Africa within fifty years. He had truly heeded the call in Romans 10:14–15: "How, then, can they call on the one they have not believed in? And how can they believe in the one of whom they have not heard? And how can they hear without someone preaching to them? And how can they preach unless they are sent?"

Meanwhile, back on the home front, one AME home missionary reported to the general conference in 1844 that during four years he had covered three hundred miles in his itinerant preaching, establishing forty-seven churches with a total membership of two thousand. He had seven other itinerant preachers working with him, and twenty-seven local preachers had organized fifty Sunday schools with two hundred teachers and two thousand students. He organized forty temperance societies and held seventeen camp meetings. One can imagine the ovation at the end of his report—one report by one missionary on fire for God.

BLACK EVANGELISM IN THE NINETEENTH CENTURY

According to historian James Stallings, the Black church engaged in evangelistic activities before the Civil War by supporting missionary personnel, founding new churches, and spearheading the abolitionist movement. During the Civil War, the Black Baptist American Convention, mainly northerners, petitioned President Lincoln and were granted permission for unofficial chaplains to accompany the Union army to evangelize their Black brothers and sisters. The Methodists also had Black chaplains accompanying the Union army. At the end of the Civil War, the Black Baptists, AMEs, and AME Zions changed the direction of their work, which heretofore had been primarily to the North. They began to evangelize the freed slaves in the South, establish new churches, and develop schools to educate the illiterate Blacks.

The disillusionment of the Reconstruction Era caused Blacks to look anew to the church as the agency of uplift and inspiration. According to Benjamin Quarles, in his book *The Negro in the Making of America* (1969), the Black independent church was freed from the controls of the White preacher or White observer that had been established during slavery. Southern Protestants divided into all White and all Black denominations. Late in 1870 the Colored Methodist Church in America separated from the Methodist Episcopal Church and organized independently. Black Southern Presbyterians formed independent churches. In 1898 the Presbyterian Church USA transferred their Black unit to a newly organized Afro-American Presbyterian church. The Episcopal church saw their colored Sunday schools disintegrate in Maryland and in the deep South by 1900. Either they became independent Black Episcopalians or they joined the Methodist or Baptist churches.

The only major denomination that escaped the color line break after the Civil War was the Catholics, largely because they started very late in evangelizing the Blacks in the South—not until 1871. According to Quarles (1969, p. 169), Carter G. Woodson described the Black preacher of this post–Civil War era as "a walking encyclopedia, the counselor of the unwise, the friend of the unfortunate, the social welfare organizer, and the interpreter of the signs of the times." The Black church was not only a soul-saving station, but a social welfare station. It became the primary source for training Blacks to handle their money and manage a business. It was the one institution that belonged to Blacks and in which they could make their own decisions.

BLACK EVANGELISM IN THE TWENTIETH CENTURY

By 1900 Black Baptists were supporting eighty elementary schools and high schools and eighteen colleges and junior colleges for educating Blacks. According to Quarles (1969), the AMEs established six colleges in sixteen years. The CME established four colleges in fourteen years; and the AME Zion founded Livingston College among other schools in the last quarter of the nineteenth century.

You may ask, "But didn't White denominations also establish schools to educate Blacks during this time?" Yes, some Whites were very sup-

portive with colleges, seminaries, and medical schools. However, I mentioned those established by independent Black denominations to illustrate that while the control of those established by Whites was in the
hands of well-meaning Whites, the control of those founded by independent Black churches was in the hands of Blacks.

While Blacks were founding schools for Christian and secular education, they were also organizing the churches for world missions.
These Blacks were so committed to African mission that one AME
bishop named Henry McNeil Turner called for the creation of a Black
Christian nation on the mother continent. Evangelism became more
and more institutionalized in the Black churches at the close of the
nineteenth century. They had a great desire to fulfill the Great Commission found in Matthew 28:19–20 to preach the gospel to every crea-
ture at home and abroad.

Black Christians saw in Jesus' teaching the opportunity for development of racial pride and autonomy. These teachings also helped them
overcome the degradation and shame of involuntary servitude and personal sinfulness. They sang their souls happy with spirituals as they
emerged. According to Lerone Bennett (1964), Black Harvard-trained
scholar W. E. B. Dubois wrote: "Rafael painted, Luther preached,
Corneille wrote, and Milton sang; and through it all for four hundred
years, the dark captives wound to the sea amid the bleaching bones of the
dead; for four hundred years the sharks followed the scurrying ships; for
four hundred years America was strewn with the living and dying millions of a transplanted race; for four hundred years Ethiopia stretched
forth her hands unto God" (p. 47).

Black evangelists at the close of the nineteenth century could point
out to those they evangelized that just as God had freed the Israelites, so
He had freed Black Israel. They weren't totally free, but they could say,
"I'm on my way to Canaan land—not an equal partner in the American
democratic form of government and not equally sharing the opportunity
of affluence in this land—but I'm on my way. If you don't go, don't hin-
der me. You can sit on the sidelines if you want to, but I am on my way,
praise God, to Canaan land."

The twentieth century came in with a blaze of glory for Blacks. By
1900 there were more than 47,000 Black professionals including 21,267
school teachers, 15,528 ministers, 1,734 medical doctors, 212 dentists,

310 journalists, 728 lawyers, 2,000 actors and showpersons, 236 artists, 247 photographers, and one Black congressperson.

Blacks had come into economic power also. In 1900 Blacks had more than $500,000 invested in funeral homes alone. By 1913, on the fiftieth anniversary of the Emancipation Proclamation, Blacks could boast of owning 550,000 homes, of operating 937,000 farms, and of conducting some 40,000 businesses. They had an accumulated wealth of over $700 million (Bennett 1964).

Over the fifty years following emancipation, the net literacy gained among Blacks was 65 percent. In 1913 there were 35,000 Black school-teachers, 1,700,000 Black pupils in public schools, and 40,000 independent Black churches. On the downside of that era were the lynchings that were taking place and the segregation laws that were being passed by cities and states. Even President Woodrow Wilson's administration joined the wave of segregation by issuing orders to racially segregate federal employees. Conditions became worse during World War I. Many of the 370,000 Black soldiers and 1,400 Black officers who fought valiantly in France were humiliated upon their return to the shores of the United States (Bennett 1964).

During the hot summer of 1919, there were twenty-six recorded race riots. The largest were in Washington, D.C.; Chicago; Omaha; Knoxville; Longview, Texas; and Philip County, Arkansas. This time Blacks were not going to take a tax on their person and on their property lying down. They fought back in defense of their personhood and their homes.

Then followed the fabulous '20s and the Black renaissance. Black artists painted, composed, published, and presented poems, plays, and musical compositions. These artists were exceptionally creative and won recognition from both the White and Black public. Such persons as Langston Hughes, Claude McKay, Countée Cullen, and James Weldon Johnson became well-known names in Black and White households. This was the era when Harlem was a mecca for Black folks. One White novelist (Carl Van Vechten) called Harlem "nigger heaven" (Bennett 1964).

Father Divine, an evangelist, though not for Jesus Christ, had one of his "heavens" in Harlem with a full-course meal for 15 cents, a clean place to lodge for 25 cents, and no collections. He had many followers.

Marcus Garvey, a Black leader from Jamaica, was a product of the '20s. He talked and dreamed big. Bennett (1964) called him a spellbinder who collected $10 million in two years. While Garvey did not evangelize for Jesus Christ, he organized cooperatives, factories, the Black Star commercial steamship line, and a private army. When White America would not heed Garvey's plea for an independent territory for Black Americans, he called on his many Black followers to go back to Africa and build a nation of their own. His efforts earned him recognition as the "Black Moses." Garvey was arrested in 1925 for mail fraud and was sentenced to five years in federal prison. Halfway through the sentence he was pardoned by President Calvin Coolidge and was deported to Jamaica in 1927. He died in obscurity in England in 1940.

Were there any Black evangelists around during this time, crying in the wilderness, "Prepare ye the way of the Lord"? Yes. For example, Edgar T. Russell, a *Pittsburgh Courier* reporter, said in the July 9, 1931, edition that some people would go so far as to assert that the Reverend George Wilson Beckton could have taken up where Marcus Garvey left off and made the back-to-Africa movement click.

Who was George Wilson Beckton? Reporter Floyd Nelson called him "the most famous evangelist of the colored race of the '20s and '30s." During the Great Depression in the 1930s when churches could not pay their bills and were on the verge of losing their buildings, God sent this strong charismatic figure to lead them into the promised land of freedom from debt. Beckton asked all who would to bring him a dime to consecrate to God. He would take these dimes home in a bag and pray over them at an altar in his home. As a result, the dimes took care of all his needs and all the needs of the churches where he held revivals. For instance, in Philadelphia, the revival was held at Tindley Temple, pastored by Charles Tindley, the famous gospel song composer. Tinley Temple was on the verge of losing their property, but the revival service conducted by Beckton, based on the giving of the consecrated dime, rescued them financially and spiritually. In fact, 2,425 new members were added to the church and $36,000 was added to the Tindley Temple treasury above regular operating expenses.

Beckton conducted similar meetings in St. Louis, Missouri, at the Tabernacle Baptist Church, where the Reverend John E. Nance was pastor. Recently, Nance's nephew, the Reverend Earl Nance, pastor of the Greater Mount Carmel Baptist Church in St. Louis, and I were discussing Beckton's revivals. He told me that "when Beckton began his revival in St.

Louis on October 1, 1931, Tabernacle was in serious financial straits and was being drained spiritually. The crowds at these revival services were overwhelming. The finances, based on the 'consecrated dimes,' made Tabernacle solvent again, and the greatest achievement was the salvation of hundreds of souls who surrendered their lives to Jesus Christ." Salem Methodist Episcopal Church in New York City, pastored by F. A. Cullen, father of the famous Black poet Countée Cullen, was similarly rescued. Over 935 persons came to Jesus during the revival in 1931. Salem Church gained $16,000 in their treasury above regular operating expenses and past indebtedness.

Let's regress a few years to 1906, when the Reverend Charles H. Mason, a Baptist minister, and two associates, D. T. Young and T. J. Jada, got word in Mississippi of a Holy Spirit experience taking place in California. They decided to go to California and see what this experience was all about. So Mason and his associates went to Azusa Street and met Brother W. J. Seymour, a Black man, who was being mightily used of God in healing and in the outpouring of the Holy Spirit upon seeking people. In fact, this Holy Ghost revival lasted for about three years. While at the Azusa Street revival, Mason and the others were filled with the Holy Spirit. Mason continued his ministry in Mississippi for a while but later went to Tennessee where he had an outstanding ministry and founded the Church of God in Christ. The Church of God in Christ today has more than three million members, with its Mason Theological Seminary being one of the five seminaries in the Interdenominational Theological Center complex in Atlanta, Georgia.

One great evangelist identified with the holiness movement was Elder "Happy Am I" (Michaux Shaw), who conducted a national radio ministry and pastored a church in Washington, D.C., with branches in New York and other cities. Many souls were saved under his fiery preaching and the enthusiastic singing of his radio choirs during the '30s and '40s.

Another renowned Black evangelist of the '30s, '40s, and '50s was William Frederick Fisher. He was an AME Zion pastor, then became ill; God restored him to health and told him to devote his life to evangelism, traveling from one city to another. He was the founder of the International Gospel Party and the Boosting Jesus Group. His powerful preaching brought thousands to Christ in such cities as Detroit, Baltimore,

Boston and Cambridge, Brooklyn, and cities in Illinois, Arkansas, Pennsylvania, and Alabama.

Other great evangelists of the twentieth century include Bishop G. T. Haywood (Pentecostal Assemblies of the World, headquarters in Indianapolis), Bishop Robert C. Lawson (Church of the Lord Jesus Christ of the Apostolic Faith, headquarters in New York City), and Bishop Smallwood E. Williams (Bibleway Church of our Lord Jesus Christ, headquarters in Washington, D.C.).

Gospel music added a powerful dimension to twentieth-century evangelism that few could resist. At first many churches did not accept gospel music with great enthusiasm, preferring to remain with the standard hymns. Despite the hesitancy of some, however, Thomas A. Dorsey, Charles Tindley, Kenneth Morris, Roberta Martin, and others were instrumental in bringing the Good News to us through gospel songs.

CONCLUSION

Today the history of Black evangelism of the '60s, '70s, '80s, and '90s is still being written. Many of the great leaders of this history-making era were in attendance at Atlanta 1988 Congress, a history-making event in itself, because of the coming together of hundreds of Black evangelists, exhorters, preachers, pastors, administrators, historians, and other leaders of many denominations, seeking a word from the Lord.

May we go forth renewed in spirit and ready to evangelize every city, town, and hamlet in our nation and in the world. May we go forth filled with the compassion that Jesus had as described in Matthew 9:35–38. In this passage He said to His disciples, "The harvest is plentiful but the workers are few." Ask the Lord of the harvest, therefore, to send out workers into his harvest field. Thank God, when the history of this period of Black evangelism is written, many of the names of those attending Atlanta 1988 Congress will be included because they said, "Here am I, Lord; send me."

REFERENCES

Bennett, L. 1964. *Before the Mayflower.* Revised edition. Chicago: Johnson.

Quarles, B. 1969. *The Negro in the making of America.* Revised Edition. New York: Collier.

Russell, E. T. 1931. *Pittsburgh weekly newspaper.* Shomburg Collection, 135th Street and Lenox Avenue, 9 July 1931.

Stallings, J. 1988. *Telling the story: Evangelism in Black churches.* Valley Forge, Pa.: Judson.

Woodson, C. G. 1921. *The history of the Negro church.* Washington, D.C.: Associated Publishers.

TOM SKINNER

Personal Reflections on Evangelism Among African-Americans

CHAPTER 2

Personal Reflections on Evangelism Among African-Americans

INTRODUCTION

I am committed to seeing the development of a technically excellent and spiritually mature generation of Christ-centered leadership. God's people have often lived at extremes of those ideals. Some people have great technical ability, are very skillful, but are spiritually out to lunch. Others are very spiritual, love the Lord, and are really gung ho, but I would not trust them to operate on me because they have not prepared themselves technically. Today we are seeing more persons who are spiritually mature and have also done their technical work. I hope that this becomes a standard for us in everything we do.

OUR CHALLENGE IN REGARD TO OUR "BLACKNESS"

In the last several years African-Americans have almost apologized for anything that has had implications to Blackness. The use of other terms, such as *minority,* has become prominent because we have become afraid to say we mean Black. This has been particularly true in the Christian community. Somehow in our theological thinking we have apologized that God would have anything to do with Blackness. We ignore it or act like it is not part of us or our heritage so as to bring about something called unity in the body of Christ. The desired result is the kind of spirit that springs from a person like the apostle Paul, who was so much in love with the Lord Jesus Christ, the gospel, and the Jewish people, that he could say, "If it is possible for me to go to hell that Israel may be saved, I am prepared to do that" (see Romans 9:3–4). I believe that in our generation there must arise young Black men and women who are so in love with Jesus, the gospel, and Black people that they would say that if going to hell could lead to the salvation of Black people, they would be prepared.

31

To love Black people is not to be against anybody. To love your redeemed Blackness is not to hate anybody. It is simply to be for yourselves and to desire for yourselves all that God has bestowed on others. Now is the time for Black Christians in this country to rise up and take our rightful place in the body of Jesus Christ and to open up ourselves and receive all that God intended for us to have.

WHAT AMERICA WAS FOUNDED TO BE

To put this into context, I remind you that America was founded to be a haven, a place of refuge for people escaping oppression in other parts of the world. Ms. Liberty stands in the New York Harbor as a shining testimony of the commitment of our country's forefathers to make America available to people seeking retreat from religious and political oppression in other parts of the world. The promise of America was that this would be the land where people could find hope. The inscription on the Statue of Liberty says it loud and clear: "Give me your tired, your poor, your huddled masses yearning to breathe free, the wretched refuse of your teeming shores. Send these, the homeless, tempest-tossed to me. I lift my lamp beside the golden door!"

But what most people missed was that while Ms. Liberty stood with her arms open facing Europe with the promise that European immigrants seeking a place of refuge in America would find it, her back was conspicuously to Harlem. Her promise did not include certain people who were already here or whose backs were being broken to build this New World.

THE INDUSTRIAL REVOLUTION

As immigrants began to pile into America, particularly into the port cities along the East coast, finally into the South, and then slowly westward in the nineteenth century, the Industrial Revolution began. The basic commodity for the Industrial Revolution was textiles, and the basic fiber for the American Revolution was cotton. A cheap form of labor had to be developed in order for the Industrial Revolution to thrive, and thus slavery was instituted.

While European immigrants were moving into the port cities of the North in great numbers, slaves in the South were working the cotton fields so that textiles could be manufactured and shipped to those port cities to be finished off and finally shipped to Europe, making America a great economic power. European immigrants built great cities along the eastern seaboard, such as Boston, New York, and Philadelphia, continuing down through the South and finally out to the West.

As these powerful industrial cities developed and wealth began to accumulate, the fourth and fifth generations of European immigrants began to move out away from the cities into what was then called the country. But the power and population remained in the cities.

THE CHANGING WHITE CHURCH AND NEIGHBORHOOD

People did not need parking lots around their churches in those days, for they had what was known as parish churches, churches that ministered to a defined community. Because the church building was centrally located in the community, parishioners could easily walk to their place of worship. But during the time preceding World War I, that began to change. From 1914 to 1916, a mass movement occurred in which 90 percent of Blacks living in the South migrated to northern cities. At the same time, Europeans began to move away from the center city to what sociologists termed "the suburbs." Nevertheless, the Europeans continued to attend their established places of worship, driving from their suburban communities into the downtown neighborhood on Sunday morning. Thus, parking lots were built.

When the Sunday morning service was over, an announcement would be made that immediately after service tea, coffee, and cookies would be served in the fellowship hall. Following the time of fellowship, the congregants would go out to the parking lot, get in their cars, and drive back to the suburbs without ever having any contact with anyone in the neighborhood. The neighborhood people never saw the churchgoers because they were still sleeping when the suburbanites arrived for worship and just rising when they left. No relationship existed between the two groups. If the downtown European church was wealthy, it was able to hire people whose ministry was to do something to reach the neighborhood people during the week.

Finally, suburbanites decided that it was too inconvenient to be driving back and forth, so they built new worship sanctuaries in their new neighborhoods. Their leaving the city churches left a great void of Christian witness in the cities.

BLACKS ENCOUNTER THE CITY

Among those people migrating into the northern cities were my own parents, who, during World War II, came up from Greenville, South Carolina, to Harlem, only to discover that the patterns of segregation were not much different from those in the South. They were faced with enormous problems in adjusting to these urban centers. One crucial issue was the lack of outreach. The problem wasn't that our communities were devoid of churches; it was that no one was organized to evangelize our communities in word and deed.

While we in Black America were not devoid of churches or preaching or spiritual witness, this throwing out of the net, this calling forth of people to a personal encounter with Jesus Christ, was not permanent among us. In fact, the gift of the evangelist was not widely known or understood.

When I was growing up, generally all preaching was done by pastors, and the only gift we knew was the gift of the pastor. Whenever we had what might have been termed "evangelistic campaigns," my father, who was a pastor, sent for a pastor from another city to preach, because evangelists were thought to be "sheep stealers." They allegedly came to town, pitched a tent, stole people from the churches, and started their own church. Therefore, anyone who was called an evangelist was suspect and not to be trusted. Thus, the gift of the evangelist did not thrive and develop among us.

Many Black pastors were truly great preachers, yet despite the majesty and theological depth of their preaching and the mighty movement of the Spirit, there was weakness in the ability to throw out the net and call people home to Jesus Christ. Instead, they opened the doors of the church and called people to membership in the institution.

EVANGELIZING FROM CRADLE TO GRAVE

Meanwhile, our European brothers and sisters ensured that their generation and succeeding generations would be able to hear the Good News from cradle to grave. Aside from their local church ministries, they developed parachurch ministries. Child Evangelism Fellowship "grabbed" young, White preschoolers and kept "hitting" them with the Word of God. When they got to school, after-school Bible clubs kept "hitting" them with the Scriptures. Then when they got to high school, they had agencies like High School Born-Againers that made sure they were developing in the things of God. Young Life sprang up to ensure that teenagers were understanding what a vibrant Christian life could be like. Youth for Christ came along and stirred young people to a commitment to Jesus Christ. When they got to college, Campus Crusade for Christ, InterVarsity, and Navigators picked them up and made sure they kept on growing. When they graduated from college, Women of Glory, Christian Businessmen, Full Gospel Businessmen, and Executive Christian Ministries "grabbed" them. Throughout a person's entire life, he or she was exposed to the gospel.

THE EVANGELISM VOID IN OUR COMMUNITIES

I went through Harlem looking for White evangelistic efforts. I also searched the south side of Chicago, the Hill district of Pittsburgh, the south and north sides of Philadelphia, and even as far west as Watts. But they were nowhere to be found. Nevertheless, I didn't hold it against them, because they were doing what they were supposed to be doing—reaching their generation and their people with the gospel. It just didn't include us.

What was more problematic was that beginning in the late 1940s, when some young African-Americans began to get interested in evangelism, they felt that the only way they could have credentials and authentically do the work of evangelism was to be hired by White agencies. They never saw that they could reach their own people with the truth of Christ on their own.

THE CHARACTER OF THE EVANGELIST

Who are these people who are going to spread the Good News of Jesus Christ in word and deed so as to influence people to put their absolute trust in Him? What sort of character will they have?

An evangelist is not a specially ordained person. Scripture makes it very clear that all of us are called to do the work of an evangelist, to have a passion for the lost. The primary requirement for effective evangelism is that one be filled with the Spirit. There is a lot of discussion about what this means and what the manifestation of the fullness of the Spirit looks like. I do not want to enter that debate, but I do want to suggest that Scripture indicates a difference between the fullness of the Spirit and the fruit of the Spirit. The Bible tells us that the evidence of the fullness of the Spirit is that one will speak the Word of God with boldness. Whenever people in Scripture were filled with the Spirit, they were fearless in their proclamation of the Good News, and people immediately identified them with Jesus.

When the apostles stood up at Pentecost, their critics recognized that they had been with Jesus. Jesus' enemies thought they had gotten rid of Him. They had nailed Him to a cross, buried Him in a tomb, rolled a stone over His grave, and then heard rumors that three days later the grave was empty. They chalked that up to Jesus' disciples stealing His body. They were not about to believe that Jesus was alive. But now they looked at Peter and saw Jesus. They looked at John and saw Jesus. They looked at the other disciples and saw Jesus. The greatest proof of the resurrection of Christ is not found in apologetics, but in people being able to see that we have been with Jesus and are filled with His Spirit. . . .

The fullness of the Spirit is that state in which a person lives in absolute abandonment to the person of Jesus Christ. It is not a state of perfection, but a state of surrender. It is not a state of sinlessness, but a state of abandonment, in which the person says, "I renounce all rights to myself and give Jesus the right to do with me whatever He pleases." It is on this point that many times we miss out on allowing the gift of evangelism to develop among us because we keep demanding the sinless part.

I remember listening to a nationally renowned preacher holding a press conference about a scandal surrounding a fellow preacher. One reporter asked whether he thought the man who had fallen would ever be able to be back in the ministry. Very emphatically the preacher responded, "No, you only get one shot at the ministry. If you blow that, that is it." I thought for a moment about all the people who would then be disqualified. We would have to take Abraham, David, and Jacob off the books along with thousands of others. But fortunately that is not the case, for the essence of the gospel is that God is at work in Christ reconciling the world to Himself. If you decide that you will abandon yourself to Jesus, He then is able to become Lord and fill you with His Spirit. God will forgive your past, so it makes no difference how often you have fallen flat on your face. It is the redeeming grace of God that gives us the privilege of being instruments in God's hands to be used with others who are filled with the Spirit and one in heart and soul.

THE DEVELOPMENT OF THE EVANGELIST

If we are going to evangelize our communities, we must develop those who are going to communicate the Good News. It doesn't make any difference whether you are going to evangelize in your profession, on street corners, in stadiums, or on radio and television. It doesn't make any difference whether you are going to do it through music, drama, or some other means that God gives you to convey it. What is important is that we develop a comradeship, a sense of family, among the people who carry the responsibility of proclaiming Good News to our generation.

Some of us will never get any recognition for what we do—no press releases, no radio or television coverage. We will do God's work simply because we have been called to do it by the King. God will put others, however, in visible arenas, which doesn't mean much other than that they will be more visible and that that visibility will bring more pain. Visibility will make them more of a target, and people will "gun" for them. We must be very careful about the potshots we take at those among us who get visibility. You may say, "Ever since he got all that national fame, he thinks he is something." Well, how do you know? Have you talked to him?

THE MESSAGE OF THE EVANGELIST

Drug addicts need Christ, but they don't need Christ because they are drug addicts. Their sin is the failure to put absolute trust in the lordship of Jesus. And until they do that, Scripture says they are dead in their sins (Ephesians 2:1). John 20:31 holds this promise: "These [things] are written that you may believe that Jesus is the Christ, the Son of God, and that by believing you may have life in his name." Sin is unbelief; it has nothing to do with being a drug addict.

So what will your message be? What will you say to people who don't drink, smoke, do drugs, fornicate, or read pornography? We need to be careful that we don't convey to them the message that because they don't do such things they don't need Jesus—that the gospel is only for bad people.

People are not sinners because they commit sins; they are sinners because they are born without the life of God. And without that life, they are incapable of being what God created them to be. Therefore, the message of the evangelist is that it is impossible to live a Christian life apart from God. The reason we hold up the Ten Commandments is so that people will see that they have come short of the glory of God. We preach about God's standards to show believers how impossible it is to live up to those standards in their own strength. But it is foolish to call nonbelievers to that standard, because they are incapable. The Christian evangelist says, "You can't live up to God's standards, but God has solved that problem by becoming a man in Jesus. Jesus has lived up to God's standards, has borne the punishment for your sins on the cross, and has risen from the dead. He is prepared to fill you with Himself. He will live His life in you without your help."

A TWO-STAGE GOSPEL

There is a two-stage gospel being preached in America. In stage one you accept Jesus as your personal Savior. You get a passport out of hell to heaven and you get the guarantee that if you die you won't go to hell. The second stage is that somewhere after that—a week, a month, or perhaps ten years later—you go to a "Deeper Life Conference" and really get into Jesus. Now the problem with this two-stage gospel is that it can't be found in Scripture. The original evangelistic message was, "If you confess with your mouth, 'Jesus is Lord,' and believe in your heart that God raised him from the dead, you will be saved" (Romans 10:9). In other words, the early evangelists made it very clear at the outset that to enter the kingdom one must abandon all that one is and all that one has to the Lord of the kingdom.

THE CONTEXT OF THE MESSAGE

What is the context of the message? Where does it get preached? Historically, the message had context only in church, and at best we hoped that we could get people to come to church to hear it. We stood on the church steps and waved people in to come hear our message. We announced the meeting by saying, "At 7:30 Sunday night the gospel will be preached in this place." The most powerful witness we gave was in church. The most wonderful testimonies I've heard were in church. The most powerful preaching I've heard was in church. And I've often thought, *Wouldn't it be wonderful if someone could give that testimony in a dugout in Yankee Stadium or at Motown Studios in Detroit or at the 21 Club? Wouldn't it be wonderful if that mighty message could be preached down in the red-light district in one of the houses of prostitution or at the local bar?*

The restriction and oppression of evangelism are due to the fact that we haven't allowed it to burst out of the four corners of our church walls. We are limited by this thing called "worldliness" because we don't want to go to the places of the world.

I have often wondered, what is a worldly place? When I have asked people that question, I have received such responses as, "A worldly place is a nightclub or place of prostitution." "A worldly place is a pornographic theater." Nobody ever says that a worldly place is the office he or she works in. Most of us don't work for Holy Spirit Computer Industries.

And most of us don't fly on TransWorld Holy Ghost Airlines. We fly on worldly airlines, ride worldly buses, and take worldly cabs driven by worldly cab drivers. We don't buy clothes at Holy Ghost Haberdashery; we buy clothes at worldly clothing stores run by worldly people. Do you know why? Because that is where God intends us to be—in the world.

Historically, we have been afraid of the world, perhaps because of the false interpretation of all those "worldly" Scriptures we were quoted: "Come out from among them ... be separate ... touch no unclean thing." But what Scripture is talking about is to come out in your conversations, in the way you live, and in your conduct even though you have to physically be in the world.

If you sprinkle salt on food, after a while all of the granules disappear because the salt goes down into the food. Nobody eats a piece of broccoli that has been salted and says, "Wow, this salt tastes awfully broccoli-like." Nobody sprinkles salt on carrots and says, "Man, this salt is really carroty." No, you say the broccoli and carrots are salty, because the salt has the ability to go into the carrots without becoming carrots. It remains salt. The salt goes down into the vegetables, rubs shoulders with them, but remains salt. Well, we say, "We can't go into the world and preach the gospel because the world will make us like them." But you just got through telling me that you are filled with the Holy Ghost and lit with the mighty fire. You just testified that you have the determination to run on and see what the end is going to be. And now you're telling me that the world is going to make you like them? You are filled with the Holy Spirit, you have on the whole armor of God—the helmet of salvation, the breastplate of righteousness, the sword of the Spirit, and the shield of faith—

and you are covered with the truth, which is the person of Jesus. Your feet are shod with the preparation of the gospel of peace, and yet you say the world is going to make you like them?

Isn't it interesting that we always talk about the way the world is going to make us. Isn't there somebody who will stand up and say, "The Spirit of the Lord is upon me, and He has anointed me to preach good news"? Instead, we say, "We can't go into those places because we might lose our testimony." How are you going to lose your testimony if you are going there to give it?

But you know what the issue is? The issue is that when we talk about losing our testimony, we are telling the truth, but not with the people we think we're talking about. What we really mean is that some gossiping Christians might see us with those people, and not understanding what we're doing, destroy our reputation with the people of God. Many of us would rather have a good reputation than to be faithful to the Word. We would rather people not talk about us than be obedient. Let me tell you something: If you are going to do the work of evangelism, people talking about you goes with the territory. You will be slandered by the wagging tongues of carnal, nonspiritual, backsliding Christians who don't have the guts to go into the world. Nevertheless, it is better to be obedient.

THE MEANING OF SPIRITUALITY

Most of us think that our spirituality is determined by the people whom we think are spiritual saying we are. So we spend all of our time trying to get them to say we are spiritual. Instead, our spiritual reputation needs to come from the non-Christian community. It is nonbelievers who must notice that we have been with Jesus. We've been building our reputation with the wrong people. Among other places, some of us need to be the salt and the light in the business world, some in the sports world, and some in the entertainment world.

THE LANGUAGE OF THE MESSAGE

People like Isaac Newton, John Newton, and Charles Wesley took the pop music of their generation and wrote the gospel to it so that the world could hear it in an idiom they understood. But we now sing those songs as if they originated from the gates of heaven. Today we have young people coming into our churches who want to evangelize their generation by communicating the gospel in the music of their generation and we call their music worldly and satanically inspired. What we must understand is that musical notes are not worldly—a B-flat is a B-flat. It is content and intent that determine what is worldly and what is righteous, and we have to learn to preach the gospel in context.

We could have been doing much more evangelizing on network television if we hadn't had the bad attitude about television we had at the close of World War II. We called it the "idiot box" and "Satan's tool," and so we missed out on the opportunity to preach on it. When the radio first came out, some Christians called it an instrument of the devil, quoting the verse that says Satan is the prince and power of the air and concluding that since radio waves travel through the air, they are obviously controlled by the devil. When Victrola first came out with phonograph records, people who played them were disfellowshiped from some churches for having an instrument of the devil in their home. It didn't occur to the people of God to grab hold of every new piece of technology and use it for the glory of God. Computers came out, and we said, "Ah, that's the tool of the Antichrist!" Some of us are still pumping out the gospel message on mimeograph machines and wondering why people don't want to read our literature, when we could be using laser printers to make it presentable.

FINANCIAL SUPPORT FOR THE EVANGELIST

We have a job to do, but who is going to pay for it? If Black people are going to reach Black people, where is the money going to come from?

If we are called to reach our generation, we have to pay for it. We are always testifying about what God saved us from, saying, "When I was in sin I used to do such and such, but God saved me from that, and I threw that away and I broke that and I burned that." Well, now that you are free from all that, you don't have to spend the money on it. Therefore, the money is free! If we would just be willing to give up some of our pleasures and excesses, we could afford to support the work of evangelism among our people.

THE NEED TO COME HOME

Some of you brothers and sisters working in White evangelistic institutions need to come home. Here is what I mean: I can name five Black people who collectively raised $8 million a year for the ministries with which they are associated, and the majority of that money went to do evangelism among non-Black people. I am not asking all Blacks to leave those institutions; I'm just saying that we are in dire need. Europeans are looking out to see that the gospel is preached among Europeans. We have catching up to do. Those of you who have built integrity and have learned fund-raising and management skills for efficiently using resources to proclaim the gospel need to come together.

PREPARING FOR WAR

Finally brothers, be strong in the Lord, because we are at war. We must equip ourselves in the Spirit to go into Satan's territory in the name of Jesus. It is not going to be easy; you are going to be shot at. Don't think that Satan is going to allow you to come into his territory and preach the Good News without a fight. Therefore, you need to put on the whole armor, and having done that, stand.

Do you know what the problem is? We have all this armor on, but we're scared of the world. We don't want to go into the world because the world might make us like them and we might lose our testimony. So instead, we duke it out with each other. We say, "I'm post[millennial], so what are you?" "Well, I'm pre[millennial]. You take that!" "I'm charismatic." "Well, I'm not. Take that!" "I was immersed." "Well, I was sprinkled. Take that!" In other words, all that is left is for us to fight among ourselves because we're scared to go into the world.

The armor is for warfare in the world, not in the body of Christ. The war is not over our methodology. It is about going into Satan's territory and turning on the light in the darkness. We need to be salt in the midst of decadence. Don't give up. Discouragements will come, but you have to keep on going if you have a passion for the lost. You have to keep on preaching and witnessing and living the life. If you put the armor on and stay faithful, loving Jesus and lifting Him up, joy will come in the morning.

PART TWO

Taking the Lead in Evangelism and Discipleship

WILLIE RICHARDSON

The Church's Role

WILLIE RICHARDSON is the pastor of Christian Stronghold Baptist Church in Philadelphia and is also the president of Christian Research and Development (CRD) of Philadelphia. Willie was a design engineer for fifteen years. He is a graduate of Philadelphia College of the Bible and serves on numerous boards. Christian Research and Development was founded in 1977 and is involved in developing the Christian family and church through seminars, conferences, retreats, and workshops. Willie has authored several workbooks, book chapters, and magazine articles, and is the author of *Reclaiming the Urban Family* (Zondervan, 1996). He is also the founder-director of the Center for Urban Resources (an organization that builds bridges and partnerships between the private sector and churches in order to improve the quality of life in the inner city). Willie has a commitment to developing pastors as managers and has done so successfully with some one hundred pastors. He was born in Florence, South Carolina, and is married to Patricia Richardson. They have four children: Gregory, Garin, Gwendolyn, and Gerald.

CHAPTER 3

WILLIE RICHARDSON

The Church's Role

INTRODUCTION

In this chapter we will examine how churches can engage in effective evangelizing and discipling. First, we will look at the need for such ministry and revisit the Great Commission. We will then seek to answer such questions as:

- What commitment must we have from the leadership of the church for effective evangelism and discipleship?
- What responsibility does the church as a whole have for evangelism and discipleship?
- How do we establish such a ministry as an ongoing force in the church?

THE NEED FOR THE MINISTRY OF EVANGELISM AND DISCIPLESHIP

We are living in a time of great discontentment. People, especially families, are seeking a better quality of life. They lack the influence of God's Word in their lives, and thus they have no guidelines for holy and happy living. Almost daily we hear of children being abused, not only by strangers, but also by their own parents. Husbands and wives seem to be in continual conflict and have an adversarial approach to the marital relationship that leaves them miserably unhappy and with their matrimonial needs unmet. A large number of single people have opted to live together without a marriage license so that it will be convenient to dump each other if the relationship doesn't work. Because of the lack of commitment, most of these relationships don't work. Those single people who do get married often select mates with such a lack of wisdom that their marriages are also doomed.

Because of the breakdown of the family and the destructive ravages of illegal drugs, more people have psychological and emotional maladies. Even when some find their way into church, churches are too often ill-equipped to deal with the deep internal conflicts that keep these people in bondage. Pastors are overwhelmed by spiritually and emotionally needy people who think the pastor should have the answer to all of their problems.

History stands as a witness that wherever Christianity has traveled, nations have been enlightened by the benefits of the church of Jesus Christ. If this is true, then what is our problem? Why does the modern church lack the power and influence of the New Testament church? My answer is that we have moved away from God's main purpose for the church.

THE GREAT COMMISSION IS STILL GREAT

Jesus came "to seek and to save what was lost" (Luke 19:10), and this is also the church's mission. When Jesus arose from the dead, appeared first to Mary Magdalene, then to the other women, and later to His male followers, He instructed them to spread the word that He would meet His followers in Galilee. This meant that when the meeting took place in Galilee, others were there besides the Twelve. As a matter of fact, Paul gives us some idea of the number of Christ's followers who were present when he says that Jesus "appeared to more than five hundred of the brothers at the same time, most of whom are still living, though some have fallen asleep" (1 Corinthians 15:6).

The instruction Jesus gave them on this grand occasion was: "Go and make disciples of all nations, baptizing them in the name of the Father and of the Son and of the Holy Spirit, and teaching them to obey everything I have commanded you. And surely I am with you always, to the very end of the age" (Matthew 28:19–20). This is what we call the Great Commission. Jesus not only commissioned the apostles, but more than five hundred people, representing all of His followers, including women, whom He had instructed along with the men to meet Him in Galilee. Thus, all believers were given this commandment. It is not an option. It is the continuation of the ministry of Jesus Christ through His body, the church. The Great Commission is a vision of a triumphant march of the church throughout the centuries, winning unbelievers to Christ and making them His disciples.

LEADERSHIP MUST BE COMMITTED TO EVANGELIZING AND DISCIPLING

Without leadership, no company, organization, or church can accomplish very much. Those who sit in the pew will not, in general, evangelize on their own. Maybe a few Christians who have a burning love for those who do not know Christ will be witnesses for the Lord. But for a church to be mobilized to evangelize and disciple others, leadership must be committed to obeying the Great Commission in its fullness.

They must be committed to making evangelism and discipleship an ongoing ministry of the church—as ongoing as the pastor giving a sermon every Sunday morning, as ongoing as the choir singing every week. It is not an optional church program. Even when every pew has been filled on Sunday morning, evangelism must be ongoing. When this happens, God will cause a church to grow spiritually and provide whatever is needed to accommodate new converts.

Evangelism and Discipleship Start with Prayer

Trying to perform ministry without prayer is an insult to God. Since the church belongs to Jesus Christ, prayer is our means of guidance and power. James 5:16–18 says: "The prayer of a righteous man is powerful and effective. Elijah was a man just like us. He prayed earnestly that it would not rain, and it did not rain on the land for three and a half years. Again he prayed, and the heavens gave rain, and the earth produced its crops."

Leadership must pray. The overall church must pray. We must pray for the Elijah kind of success if we want to produce crops of new converts for the Lord Jesus Christ. We must pray for evangelistic opportunities, for the salvation message to be made clear and plain; and for ourselves to conduct our lives in an exemplary way, manifesting the character of Christ. Such were the prayer requests of the New Testament church leaders:

> Devote yourselves to prayer, being watchful and thankful. And pray for us, too, that God may open a door for our message, so that we may proclaim the mystery of Christ, for which I am in chains. Pray that I may proclaim it clearly, as I should. Be wise in the way you act toward outsiders; make the most of every opportunity. Let your conversation be always full of grace, seasoned with salt, so that you may know how to answer everyone. (Colossians 4:2–6)

Goals Motivate

God is a planner and goal-setter. For example, Ephesians 1:4–5 tells us, "He chose us in him before the creation of the world to be holy and blameless in his sight. In love he predestined us to be adopted as his sons through Jesus Christ, in accordance with his pleasure and will."

We, likewise, need to set goals for our evangelistic endeavors. First, we need to take notice of the geographic strategy that Jesus gave the apostles to carry out His Great Commission: "You will receive power when the Holy Spirit comes on you; and you will be my witnesses in Jerusalem, and in all Judea and Samaria, and to the ends of the earth" (Acts 1:8). We must depend on the Holy Spirit to empower us to share our faith starting in "Jerusalem"—that is, our home. The church must reach its own neighborhood and the unsaved relatives of church members with the claims of Christ. In the early church entire families were reached for Christ. When a violent earthquake shook the Philippian jail where Paul and Silas were incarcerated, the jailer asked them, "'What must I do to be saved?' They replied, 'Believe in the Lord Jesus, and you will be saved—you and your household.' Then they spoke the word of the Lord to him and to all the others in his house" (Acts 16:30–32).

Next we must reach our "Judea and Samaria," our city, town, or county. We are in a mobile society where people come and go in communities. One of the reasons some churches do not grow numerically is because they do not stay in touch with their neighborhood. The church must know who its new neighbors are.

Finally, we must accept our responsibility to reach the world through foreign and home missions efforts. Our mission for Christ is not complete until the church moves beyond self-interest to getting nothing in return except satisfaction that we are obeying and doing God's will.

Training for an Ongoing Ministry of Evangelism and Discipleship

When developing an evangelistic ministry, the key to its success is to train people in small groups, because the training itself is a form of discipleship. We first make disciples of our existing members. It is especially good if the pastor personally recruits church members for this ministry by sharing the vision for evangelism and discipleship.

The following steps should be considered in training:

1. Begin training with the pastor preaching a series of messages from God's Word, giving an understanding of what the Great Commission means. During the sermon series, it should be announced that a class will be taught on how Christians share their faith, enabling them to be obedient to Christ.

2. Follow the sermons with a class on how to share your faith with unbelievers. To be a good witness for Christ, we must know how to communicate the salvation message.

Aldrich (1993, p. 79) points out the importance of communicating the salvation message along with cultivating a relationship.

> Cultivating establishes the validity of what is proclaimed. Relationship alone is not enough. No one is good enough to let just his life speak for Christ. Words are necessary to point beyond himself to Christ. Nevertheless, the unbeliever needs to *feel* the impact of the good news that Christ loves people, and not merely listen to it. When love is *felt* the message is heard. Gut relationship which never leads to sowing is an extreme to be avoided. We are fishers of men sent to catch fish, not frogmen who swim with the fish, making our presence known. A healthy relationship increases the impact of the gospel's revelation because it helps people to perceive the gospel as good news.

Christians should be taught how to use a few Scriptures in a salvation plan such as "The Romans Road":

Our sinful and unrighteous condition—Romans 3:10, 23
God's love—Romans 5:8
The need for salvation—Romans 5:12
The free gift in Christ—Romans 6:23
Salvation in Christ—Romans 10:9–10

Such training should be included in the church's new members' class. Role playing is an effective witnessing training technique.

3. Teach students how to deal with the objections and excuses of unbelievers. Not knowing how to deal with objections and excuses will hamper the success of a person who witnesses for the Lord.

4. Train believers in Christ to be students of God's Word. The mature soul winner should know sound biblical doctrine and know how to introduce Jesus Christ by using the Bible.

5. Follow up on new converts to establish them in the faith and to assimilate them into the body of Christ. This is where many who evangelize fall short. The new convert must become a member of the local church in order to grow, be cared for by a pastor as well as by other believers, and become a productive, spiritual Christian.

6. Assign the trainees to evangelism teams made up of small groups of soul winners who have been given evangelistic projects (see below).

EVANGELISM METHODS

"Go and make disciples. . ." (Matthew 28:19). We can learn how to evangelize by sharing our faith, but if we don't "go"—if we don't actually witness to nonbelievers—we have failed and are in disobedience to God. We must do it! We must engage in spiritual warfare and rescue lost people from the kingdom of darkness ("open their eyes and turn them from darkness to light, and from the power of Satan to God," Acts 26:18).

Below are some effective ways for a church to evangelize nonbelievers.

1. *Relational evangelism.* This is the most effective of all methods. Most people come to Christ because of their relationship with a Christian, whether that person be a relative, coworker, neighbor, fellow student, sports teammate, fellow volunteer, or business associate. This is why it is essential that every member of the church know how to share his or her faith in Jesus Christ.

2. *Inviting and bringing nonbelievers to church on a Sunday morning.* This is effective if the pastor presents a clear application of Scripture to everyday living and gives a salvation invitation at the end of the sermon.

3. *Individual Christians sharing their faith at family gatherings (reunions, weddings, funerals, etc.).*

4. *Church family and friends Sunday.* This is a special Sunday service to which a special effort is made to invite unsaved family members and friends. The message should be geared to this type of attendance.

5. *Evangelistic services.* Invite to your church for a series of meetings an evangelist who has the gift of winning souls to Christ.

6. *Small-group evangelistic Bible study.* Structure small Bible studies that have salvation as their primary emphasis.

7. *Door-to-door evangelism.* Establish a specific time when members team up and visit homes to present the salvation message.

8. *Youth evangelism.* Develop programs aimed specifically at presenting the salvation message to youth.

9. *Child evangelism.* Develop programs geared specifically for leading children to Christ.

10. *Male/female evangelism.* The unique issues males face are considered in male evangelism. For specific tips in this area, see Richardson (1991). For females, our special focus is on areas such as prison, drug addiction, and female single parents.

11. *Family evangelism.* This approach considers the critical issues families face and draws upon the Scriptures in framing the message. In this approach, unsaved families can be visited or worked with until all members are presented with the gospel. We first reach one family member, and that member is trained in how to share his or her faith with others. This person then focuses on reaching everyone else in the family for Christ. Additionally, all church families are encouraged to befriend their unsaved neighbors and friends as a way of spreading God's love and reaching families for Christ.

12. *Telephone evangelism.* A telethon may be arranged at the church, wherein unsaved persons who have indicated an openness to the gospel, via visitor cards or other means, are called and presented with the salvation message. One could also assign names of persons to call from their own homes. We also use this as a way to familiarize those in the community with our church and God's message.

DISCIPLING

Evangelism is incomplete if it does not flow naturally into discipleship. Discipling is seeing that the new convert is rooted and grounded in the faith. The apostle Paul said, "Just as you received Christ Jesus as Lord, continue to live in him, rooted and built up in him, strengthened in the faith as you were taught, and overflowing with thankfulness" (Colossians 2:6–7).

We who have embraced Jesus Christ as Lord and Savior and have committed ourselves to following Him are disciples. We in turn are called to make disciples. Hull (1990, pp. 20–21) describes this undertaking:

Every disciple should make disciples. Jesus gave the command to the apostles, who represented the best and worst of mankind—you might call them mankind in microcosm. Because we have the same ability and responsibility as the original disciples, every contemporary disciple is no less capable of this calling than the twelve.

Disciple making includes introducing people to Christ, building them up in faith, and sending them into the harvest field. This process can be summarized by what I call the three Ds of disciple making: *Deliver them, develop them,* and *deploy them.*

Through the power of Christ we are delivered from sin; by the discipling process we are developed into mature believers; finally God deploys us into the harvest field to reach others. Some disciples will have leadership gifts, and God will call them to spearhead the disciple-making activity. Only a few are called to leadership in the corporate body, but every disciple should take part in the disciple-making process at some level. . . .

Jesus told the disciples to make as many disciples in as many places as they could and promised He would be with them until "the very end of the age." Christ knew the mission would outlive those men, and we have not yet reached the end of the age. Therefore, Jesus' instructions remain in force today as much as they did the day He issued them. Making disciples will continue until Christ comes again. The church of Jesus Christ is under orders to keep on making disciples as long as we have breath. This is the driving force and foundation of all the church is and does.

Some Discipling Methods

Below are six methods of discipling that have proven successful.

1. *Expository preaching.* Some discipling takes place when the pastor gives expository sermons that teach and apply the Word of God.
2. *New members' class.* Taught by the pastor (if possible), these classes are key to establishing a new Christian in the faith. Another variation of this is a small group designed to teach new members.
3. *Mentoring.* A new member can be mentored by a mature Christian.

4. *Following up with inactive church members.* This is a very important aspect of discipling. As Christians, we are constantly involved in spiritual warfare with Satan. Christians are challenged to be vigilant in watching and praying for each other. "Pray in the Spirit on all occasions with all kinds of prayers and requests. With this in mind, be alert and always keep on praying for all the saints" (Ephesians 6:18). A sister or brother in Christ may have been caught in Satan's trap and may need the assistance of a strong mature Christian.
5. *Discipleship groups.* These are groups of four to twelve people designed with the objective of helping Christians grow spiritually in a small-group setting.
6. *Care groups.* Care groups are formed for the purpose of meeting some special need in the life of a particular group of people, such as new parents, stepparents, single parents, alcoholics, widows and widowers, etc.

EVANGELISM AND DISCIPLING RESOURCES

Because evangelism and discipling are too often neglected in the Christian church, over the years we have been hard pressed to find current books and other resources. Many resources are authored by seminary and university professors who present a theoretical point of view that may be untested and impractical in ministry. This has prompted our local church to produce resources to use in our ministry, which we have made available to others through Christian Research and Development. Some of the best resources available are listed here:

Aldrich, Joe. *Lifestyle Evangelism* (Sisters, Ore.: Questar, 1993). Gives great understanding of relational evangelism and why it is so effective.

Hull, Bill. *The Disciple Making Pastor* (Old Tappan, N.J.: Revell, 1988) and *The Disciple Making Church* (Old Tappan, N.J.: Revell, 1990). Challenges pastors and churches to obey the biblical mandate to carry out the ministry of evangelism and discipling.

June, Lee N., editor. *The Black Family: Past, Present and Future* (Grand Rapids: Zondervan, 1991). Has a chapter on how to evangelize men and is also an excellent tool for discipling and developing families.

Richardson, Willie. *Reclaiming the Urban Family* (Grand Rapids: Zondervan, 1996). Includes not only instruction on how to evangelize families, but also directions for establishing an ongoing ministry to families.

The following resources are produced by Christian Research and Development, 27 W. Township Line Road, Upper Darby, PA 19083. Phone 1-800-5511-CRD.

Richardson, Patricia. 1998. *Women of Great Price.* A two-phase program for discipling women. Instructor's kit consists of a leader's guide, a disciple's workbook, an instructor's audiocassette, and a booklet on soul winning.

Richardson, Willie. 1998. *Being a Witness for the Lord.* Booklet instructs the individual Christian in how to lead others to Christ by sharing his or her faith as a way of life.

_____. 1994. *Crowned with Glory and Honor.* An evangelistic tool.

_____. 1994. *Glory and Honor.* Designed for small-group follow-up.

_____. 1994. *A Plan for Getting More Men into the Church and Keeping Them.* A how-to book on planning and establishing an evangelism and discipleship ministry in the local church to reach males in the community. Strategies found in this book can be adapted to reach people in general.

_____. 1984. *Making Jesus King.* A two-phase program (fifteen weeks each) for discipling men. Instructor's kit consists of a leader's guide, a disciple's workbook, an instructor's audiocassette, a booklet on soul winning, and men's surveys used for reaching men in the community.

CONCLUSION

The church is God's lifeline to the world. The church is the world's second chance to please God. The church must give unconverted people the opportunity to die once and live twice by receiving eternal life through Jesus Christ, or the world will die twice and live once, the second death being spent in eternal suffering. Revelation 20:6 says, "Blessed and holy are those who have part in the first resurrection. The second death has no power over them, but they will be priests of God and of Christ and will reign with him for a thousand years." To accomplish the Great Commission and to keep people from having to face this second death, the church must evangelize and disciple others as a way of life.

REFERENCES

Aldrich, J. 1993. *Lifestyle evangelism.* Sisters, Ore.: Questar.

Hull, B. 1990. *The disciple making church.* Old Tappan, N.J.: Revell.

_____. 1988. *The disciple making pastor.* Old Tappan, N.J.: Revell.

June, L. N., ed. 1991. *The Black family: Past, present and future.* Grand Rapids: Zondervan.

Richardson, P. 1998. *Women of great price.* Philadelphia: Christian Research and Development.

Richardson, W. 1998. *Being a witness for the Lord.* Philadelphia: Christian Research and Development.

_____. 1996. *Reclaiming the urban family.* Grand Rapids: Zondervan.

_____. 1994a. *Crowned with glory and honor.* Philadelphia: Christian Research and Development.

_____. 1994b. *Glory and honor.* Philadelphia: Christian Research and Development.

_____. 1994c. *A plan for getting more men in the church and keeping them.* Philadelphia: Christian Research and Development.

_____. 1991. Evangelizing Black males: Critical issues and how-to. In *The Black family: Past, present and future.* Edited by L. N. June. Grand Rapids: Zondervan.

_____. 1984. *Making Jesus king.* Philadelphia: Christian Research and Development.

LLOYD C. BLUE

The Pastor's Role

LLOYD C. BLUE is chief executive officer of Church Growth Unlimited, headquartered in Mendenhall, Mississippi, and is the former pastor of North Oakland Missionary Baptist Church in Oakland, California. He is nationally acclaimed for his lectures in the areas of personal evangelism, ministry of the Holy Spirit, abundant Christian living, building disciples, church growth, family enrichment, pastoral management and counseling, the mechanics of expository preaching, and methods for city- or statewide revival meetings. He attended California Baptist College, received his bachelor of theology degree from the Institutional Baptist Theological Center, Houston, master of arts degree from Union University in Los Angeles, and a doctor of ministry degree from the University of Central America. A native of North Carolina, Lloyd is married to Tressie Blue. They have one son, Lloyd II, and two adopted daughters, Kay and Robbin.

CHAPTER 4

LLOYD C. BLUE

The Pastor's Role

It was [Christ] who gave some to be apostles, some to be prophets, some to be evangelists, and some to be pastors and teachers, to prepare God's people for works of service, so that the body of Christ may be built up until we all reach unity in the faith and in the knowledge of the Son of God and become mature, attaining to the whole measure of the fullness of Christ.

Ephesians 4:11–13

INTRODUCTION

The biblical role of the pastor-teacher is crystal clear. In Ephesians 4:11 pastors and teachers do not identify two but rather one person with a dual characterization. The pastor is much like a player-coach, in that the player-coach plays just like the other players with the same responsibility to win but is also responsible for giving instruction and developing the skills of the team so they may be prepared to win the game.

One person—the player-coach. This is a concept also discussed by Hull (1988). The responsibility of the players is to win while the responsibility of the coach is to train and instruct the players in how to win. The responsibility of the pastor-teacher, as stated in Ephesians 4:12, is "to prepare God's people for works of service, so that the body of Christ may be built up." As in the case of the player-coach, the pastor-teacher must do the work of ministry and then, as teacher, train and instruct the saints in how to do the work of ministry (that is, equip them). One person—pastor-teacher—for the "perfecting" (KJV) of God's people. This is a tremendous position, because perfecting means "to make fit, to complete, to mend, to equip, to put in order." Therefore, pastor-teachers must view themselves as God's means for the perfecting of the saints, that is, for equipping them

61

for Christian service. Not just anyone can perform this task; only the God-called pastor-teacher can do this work successfully. Therefore, to be successful, such a person must have the assurance of at least three things:

- Eternal life
- The calling to serve as pastor-teacher
- The ministering work of the Holy Spirit

Each of these will be discussed independently for clarification.

ASSURANCE OF ETERNAL LIFE

If you are sure of your own eternal life in Christ, there is no need for you to feel insulted by this section, but rather thank God for the blessed assurance that you are His child and that Jesus Christ is living in you.

However, if you are not sure, you are not the first and you will not be the last person in the role of pastor-teacher who has faced up to this fact. This is a very serious matter that should not be taken lightly, because it is very difficult to give to another what you are not sure you have.

I will now explain how you can be sure of your salvation by believing the truth of God's Word.

Truth #1   God loves you.

God so loved the world that he gave his one and only Son, that whoever believes in him shall not perish but have eternal life. (John 3:16)

God demonstrates his own love for us in this: While we were still sinners, Christ died for us. (Romans 5:8)

God proved His love for us when He gave His only begotten Son to die in our place.

Truth #2   All have sinned.

All have sinned and fall short of the glory of God. (Romans 3:23)

If we claim to be without sin, we deceive ourselves and the truth is not in us. (1 John 1:8)

We are born into this world less than God created us to be and must be born again.

Truth #3   *Sin separates us from God.*

The wages of sin is death, but the gift of God is eternal life in Christ Jesus our Lord. (Romans 6:23)

As in Adam all die, so in Christ all will be made alive. (1 Corinthians 15:22)

In Adam we all died (were separated from God), but in Christ we are all made alive (reconciled to God).

Truth #4   *We are reconciled to God by receiving Jesus Christ.*

I stand at the door and knock. If anyone hears my voice and opens the door, I will come in and eat with him, and he with me. (Revelation 3:20)

To all who received him, to those who believed in his name, he gave the right to become children of God. (John 1:12)

When we by faith invite Christ to come into our lives, the life we lost in Adam is restored and we become children of God.

The thief comes only to steal and kill and destroy; I have come that they may have life, and have it to the full. (John 10:10)

We can by faith and through prayer invite Jesus Christ to come into our lives, and He will come in just as He promised.

He then brought them out and asked, "Sirs, what must I do to be saved?" They replied, "Believe in the Lord Jesus, and you will be saved—you and your household." (Acts 16:30–31)

Note the question the Philippian jailer asked: "Sirs, what must I do to be saved?" Now observe the answer: "Believe in the Lord Jesus, and you will be saved—you and your household." You cannot have Jesus Christ as Savior until you acknowledge Him as Lord. Note very carefully what these next verses say.

This is the testimony: God has given us eternal life, and this life is in his Son. He who has the Son has life; he who does not have the Son of God does not have life. I write these things to you who believe in the name of the Son of God so that you may know that you have eternal life. (1 John 5:11–13)

When you acknowledge Jesus Christ as Lord and receive Him into your life as Savior, you have eternal life because eternal life is in Him. John says that this is written so that we may *know* that we have eternal life. By faith in God and His Word we *know* that we have eternal life.

ASSURANCE OF YOUR CALLING TO SERVE AS PASTOR-TEACHER

Salvation is a dynamic call from God. It is entirely of the Lord. No one can make himself or herself a Christian. Likewise, I am convinced that there is a special call to pastor that only the person called can really know and understand.

The one thing that caused me to wait for seven years to respond to God's call to preach and eventually pastor was that it did not make sense to me. My thinking was, how could God need someone so badly that He would call someone so unprepared? It never dawned on me that God was concerned about my availability and not my ability and that He was prepared to do in me and through me what He was demanding of me, just as He did with Moses at the burning bush (Exodus 3). The extraordinary need for Bible preaching in our society today is not a reason to volunteer. Recall that the Twelve did not volunteer; on the contrary, it was the magnetic authority of the Lord that compelled them. The reality of the call could not be resisted.

Mark 1:16–18 says: "As Jesus walked beside the Sea of Galilee, he saw Simon and his brother Andrew casting a net into the lake, for they were fishermen. 'Come, follow me,' Jesus said, 'and I will make you fishers of men.' At once they left their nets and followed him." A little further on in Mark 2:14 we read: "As he walked along, he saw Levi son of Alphaeus sitting at the tax collector's booth. 'Follow me,' Jesus told him, and Levi got up and followed him." And Luke 5:9–11 records: "[Simon Peter] and all his companions were astonished at the catch of fish they had taken, and so were James and John, the sons of Zebedee, Simon's partners. Then Jesus said to Simon, 'Don't be afraid; from now on you will catch men.' So they pulled their boats up on shore, left everything and followed him."

The call of our Lord is strong and lifelong. We must respect the sovereignty of God, who calls, gifts, and anoints whom He wills to preach His Word. The old-timers used to say, "Preach when you can't help it." I think that's what Paul had in mind when he said, "I am compelled to preach. Woe to me if I do not preach the gospel!" (1 Corinthians 9:16).

Time and time again it was the strength of the call that helped the leaders of the church maintain their courage and confidence. You will know when it is time to respond.

ASSURANCE OF THE MINISTERING WORK OF THE HOLY SPIRIT

Dr. Timothy J. Winters, senior pastor of Bayview Baptist Church of San Diego, said in a sermon that "we are anointed by the Holy Spirit at the time of the new birth, at which time we are also called and gifted to do a particular task" (1966). Paul speaks of this anointing in 2 Corinthians 1:21–22: "It is God who makes both us and you stand firm in Christ. He anointed us, set his seal of ownership on us, and put his Spirit in our hearts as a deposit, guaranteeing what is to come."

Many things happened to me at the time of the new birth. When I got saved, I was established (2 Corinthians 1:21) and I was sealed (v. 22). That means that I am as good as in heaven. I have received the earnest of the Spirit (v. 22), which means that I have the down payment on my future. I was also anointed (v. 21). The anointing is a work of the Holy Spirit empowering us to do the task God called and gifted us to do. Although we are anointed at the new birth, a special anointing will come upon us when needed. For example, when a pastor receives the anointing in the pulpit, the Holy Spirit gives that pastor supernatural empowerment. We can explore this a little further by examining 1 John 2:20, 27 (NASB): "You have an anointing from the Holy One, and you all know. . . . And as for you, the anointing which you received from Him abides in you, and you have no need for anyone to teach you; but as His anointing teaches you about all things, and is true and is not a lie, and just as it has taught you, you abide in Him."

Since every believer has an anointing, it is important that we understand the purpose for it. First, we know all things (1 John 2:20). This does not mean we know everything about everything, but it does mean that we can discern the truth from a lie. When we hear a lie, the Holy Spirit lets us know it. If anyone needs to be able to detect error, it is the pastor-teacher.

Second, God's anointing teaches us about all things (1 John 2:27). This does not mean that we know all truth, but nothing is hidden from Him, and thus He can teach us the truth. If you will let Him, the Holy Spirit will teach you everything you need to know about being the kind of pastor-teacher you need to be. Stay in the Word of God, and the Holy Spirit, who is the Truth, will teach you the truth.

Having observed the assurances the pastor-teacher must have, we will now consider the pastor-teacher in reference to passion, perception, pursuit, preparation, plan, performance, preaching and teaching, and perspective.

THE PASTOR-TEACHER AND PASSION

As pastor-teacher you must have an intense driving conviction to fulfill your role of "preparing God's people for works of service" (evangelism and discipleship). Passion is an emotional thing, and whatever controls your emotions will direct your will. Whatever directs your will, will govern your behavior. Therefore, if you do not have a passion to see men and women living the abundant life and discipling others, evangelism and discipleship will never become the central focus of your ministry.

Paul writes in Philippians 1:20, "I eagerly expect and hope that I will in no way be ashamed, but will have sufficient courage so that now as always Christ will be exalted in my body, whether by life or by death." Clearly the only thing that mattered to Paul was that Christ be magnified in his body, whether it be by his life or his death. In the same manner, you must have a passion for preparing God's people to do the work of ministry. If your passion does not reach the level that Paul had, it will not take much to stop you.

THE PASTOR-TEACHER AND PERCEPTION

As pastor-teacher, you must perceive yourself to be the only person on the planet God has called, gifted, and anointed to prepare His people to do the work of ministry in your local church. However, to be called, gifted, and anointed is not enough. You must have a vision big enough to see beyond the boundaries of the traditional local church. You must set your focus on Christ until "all reach unity in the faith and in the knowledge of the Son of God and become mature, attaining to the whole measure of the fullness of Christ" (Ephesians 4:13). This is one of the most comprehensive utterances ever made by the apostle Paul. It describes the conclusion of the battle, the end of the race, and the climax of everything attempted by God in the formation, growth, and purification of the church. When we think about becoming spiritually mature, we think about the Lord Jesus, the only perfect person since Adam's fall. He is not only without sin, but is incapable of improvement—something we will never be in our own righteousness. Nevertheless, Paul indicates that only a vision for persons to attain to the whole measure of the fullness of Christ is big enough to get excited about.

You must challenge your church to return to its first calling. Look at the universal church and the local church through a discerning scriptural lens and think systematically concerning objectives and methods. You must place people in programs, ministries, and so on according to their gifts and for their spiritual growth and development. You must keep your vision on "becoming mature, attaining to the whole measure of the fullness of Christ."

Because the church has stumbled so far from its prescribed purpose and methods, people now consider a call to fulfill the Great Commission revolutionary. When we read through the book of Acts, we must recognize that the church at its birth was the church at its best. If we are going to call the church to be the church at its best, we must be revolutionary in our thinking. Nothing less is big enough to cause the church to commit to change, and change it must.

If the local church pastor-teacher does not have a vision for "becoming mature, attaining to the whole measure of the fullness of Christ," the pastor-teacher will not have a commitment for "preparing God's people for works of service." The lack of such a vision results in thinking of the church as existing for itself. Without the right vision, the challenge to the members becomes merely, "Commit yourself to the church, build it up, and make it the focal point of your Christian experience." This pastor-teacher whose focus is on only the ministry of the church to the church will seek to keep the members happy and enjoy a good reputation with other churches. The highest calling in this church is to be all you can be in the church. And if you are faithful in attendance and bring your tithe, you can work your way up to be president, chairperson, trustee, or even a deacon.

I will never forget the time I was given a set of questions and answers to memorize for the big day when I would be ordained to serve as a deacon. Well, my big day came and went, and after it was all over, the only difference was that before I was just a carnal choir member, and after I was a carnal deacon singing in the choir.

Dearly beloved, I plead with you to change your focus from being a local church thinker to a revolutionary thinker. Set your sights on "becoming mature, attaining to the whole measure of the fullness of Christ," so that you and your people will be motivated to "prepare God's people for works of service, so that the body of Christ may be built up until we all reach unity in the faith."

You may be asking why I would write this kind of indictment against local church leadership. Well, I'm glad you asked, because for more than thirty years I was guilty of all of the above. I write this now in the hope that you will not wait until your thirtieth year to look back over your life and think about how much more you could have done for the kingdom of God. No matter what others say about me and what I was able to accomplish, I will always know that it could have been so much more. And I must one day stand before Almighty God and give an account of the deeds I did and did not do.

THE PASTOR-TEACHER AND PURSUIT

As pastor-teacher, you must get beyond merely talking about evangelism and discipleship and dedicate yourself to making it the central focus of the church. If you remain focused on traditional programs and lose sight of the Lord's purpose and goals for His church, the needs of your people will go unmet and they will never know the reality of serving the Lord.

As I minister across the country, the questions asked by church people have caused me to conclude that some of the most critical unmet needs in the lives of Christians are due to their not understanding the following:

- The assurance of salvation (John 1:12; 1 John 5:11–13)
- How to deal with sin the moment they become aware of it (1 John 1:9)
- The assurance of victory (1 Corinthians 10:13)
- How, by faith, to appropriate the fullness of the Holy Spirit—the Christ-controlled life (Ephesians 5:8; 1 John 5:14–15)
- How to walk in Christ as they have received Him by faith (Colossians 2:6–10)
- How to live in Christ's strength (Philippians 2:13; 4:13; 1 Thessalonians 5:24)

- How to witness in the power of the Holy Spirit (Acts 1:8)
- How to communicate the claims of Christ to others in a clear, contemporary way (Mark 5:19; Romans 10:14)
- How they can be involved in evangelism and still genuinely be themselves (Matthew 4:19)
- How to pray with confidence (John 14:12–14; 15:7; 16:24; 1 John 5:14–15)
- How to love every person (1 John 3:16–20; 4:11–12)
- How to receive God's directions (2 Chronicles 20:1–20; Proverbs 3:5–6)
- God's purpose for the local church (Matthew 28:18–20; Mark 16:15)
- How to study the Bible (Joshua 1:8; Psalm 119:9–16; Acts 17:11; 2 Timothy 3:16–17)
- The experience of stimulation and accountability in a close spiritual fellowship with other members of the body of Christ (Acts 2:46; Hebrews 10:25)
- The necessity of putting Christ first (Matthew 6:33)
- How to worship and praise God (Revelation 4:9–11)
- How to give God's way (Malachi 3:7–12; Luke 6:38; 1 Corinthians 16:1–2; 2 Corinthians 9:7)
- The value of the church assembly (Psalm 122:1; Matthew 18:19–20; Hebrews 10:25)
- Christian mission (Acts 10)
- How to manage their time and the gifts of the Holy Spirit (Matthew 25:14–30)

Your people need to know that they are an important part of a workable plan designed to involve all church members in eventually reaching all non-Christians in their community. Without this vision they will not have a real sense of the church's mission. They cannot help feeling hypocritical if they are not vitally involved in what is so clearly God's priority for the church (see Proverbs 29:18). Teaching and presenting the above is essential to the process of equipping God's people to do the work of ministry.

THE PASTOR-TEACHER AND PREPARATION

As pastor-teacher you must be aware of the inherent value of what you already have in your church. One of the most encouraging facts is that preparing God's people to do the work of ministry does not require a whole new church organizational structure. Careful study will reveal that ministries to meet these needs can be implemented through three areas of the church's organizational structure: the pulpit, the Christian education department, and the discipleship/evangelism department.

The Pulpit

Your pulpit presentation is vital to the process of preparing God's people to do the work of ministry. Therefore, expository preaching is a must. We are commanded to "preach the Word" (2 Timothy 4:2), and expository preaching is Bible-centered, instructional preaching, expounding Scripture as a unified body of truth. It brings listeners into the presence of God and creates a dialogue for healthy change.

The Christian Education Department

You must make sure that your Christian education department is also designed to prepare God's people to do the work of ministry. If workers enter your Christian education department and are faithful for four or five years, they should be faithfully reproducing themselves in others. If this is not true for you, something is wrong with your Christian education department.

The Discipleship/Evangelism Department

Most churches do not have a discipleship/evangelism department because either no one is being equipped in the Christian education department to do the work of ministry (discipleship/evangelism) or this is not a priority. If this is true of your church, now is the time to remedy the situation.

THE PASTOR-TEACHER AND A PLAN

Before you begin your plan, you should thoroughly evaluate how all your church activities can contribute to preparing God's people to do the work of ministry and to evangelizing all the non-Christians in your community. Planning is predetermining a course of action, and the saying is true, "One who fails to plan, plans to fail." Develop a plan with ministries that will most effectively nurture the Christ dependence of your members and help your church fulfill its purpose.

Be willing to implement the necessary steps, under the guidance of the Holy Spirit, to supplement the existing ministries of the church and as necessary to revise existing activities so they can help fulfill the priorities.

Prepare to apply all energy, training, finances, and talent toward fulfilling God's purpose and goal for His church. Your church can have a spiritual awakening and your community can be saturated with the Good News about Christ, but it will be in direct proportion to the number of your members that are living in the resurrection power of Jesus Christ and effectively sharing their faith as a way of life wherever they live, work, and play.

THE PASTOR-TEACHER AND PERFORMANCE

To perform well and achieve lasting results, there are sixteen "musts" you cannot disregard. Therefore, you must:

1. Know that you are accountable to God for your stewardship (Matthew 25:14–30; Hebrews 13:7).
2. Understand that evangelizing and discipling is not an option (Matthew 28:18–20).
3. Be committed, gifted, and enabled by God to equip the saints to do the work of the ministry (Romans 12:4–8; Ephesians 4:11–16).
4. Understand that God enables what He requires (Philippians 2:13; 4:13; Colossians 1:29; 1 Thessalonians 5:24).
5. Understand that unity from abiding in Christ allows God-given diversity to flow (John 15:4–8; Ephesians 4:11–16).
6. Understand that the Lord ministers through His disciples (Galatians 2:20; 5:22–24; Ephesians 5:18).
7. Understand that Christians are redeemed to serve (1 Corinthians 15:58; Ephesians 2:10; Hebrews 10:24).
8. Understand that disciples (not programs) make disciples (Luke 6:40; 2 Timothy 2:2).
9. Understand that the heart of discipleship is self-death that results in submission to Christ and dependence upon Him as Lord (Luke 9:23–25; 1 Corinthians 9:24–27).
10. Concentrate on those who are responsive to your ministry (Matthew 13:1–23; Luke 8:4–15).
11. Select leaders carefully and prayerfully (1 Timothy 5:22).
12. Start with a manageable size group (Luke 14:28).

13. Develop effectiveness first (Proverbs 4:25–27).
14. Expand at the rate that you have qualified, committed, and available leadership (2 Timothy 2:2).
15. Understand that disciples are those who are faithful, available, and teachable (2 Timothy 2:15–16; Hebrews 13:17).
16. Understand that all honor and praise for achievement belong to God (Psalm 127:1; 1 Corinthians 1:26–31).

THE PASTOR-TEACHER AND PREACHING AND TEACHING

What you preach is as important as how you preach. As pastor-teacher you must build a Great Commission vision for your church by preaching and teaching biblical principles. Church members must understand that this means:

- Accepting the Bible as final authority (Matthew 5:18; 1 Peter 1:25)
- Seeing people who are outside Christ as lost (Luke 19:9–10)
- Affirming that God's love and concern are for all people (John 3:16; Romans 5:8; 1 Timothy 2:3–4)
- Believing that Christ is the only way (John 14:5–6)
- Obedience to the leading of the Holy Spirit (John 16:12–13)
- Praying intelligently and specifically for the growth of the church (Jeremiah 33:3)
- Seeing the church as the body of Christ (Romans 12:4–5; 1 Corinthians 12:12–31)
- Holding the church to be a necessary part of God's plan for the salvation and discipling of all humankind (Matthew 28:19–20)

We must not only believe in Jesus Christ, but must become responsible members of His church. The Bible requires that, and if we take the Bible seriously, we cannot hold any other viewpoint. Churches that wish to grow must respect biblical principles or they will go astray in mere activism, statistical concern, or self-glorification. But when they do respect biblical principles, they can press forth under our sovereign God to vigorous growth, conscious that they are in God's will and that what they are doing is pleasing to God. You must also preach and teach:

- That the church is at the heart of God's plan for reaching the world (Matthew 28:18–20; Mark 16:15)

- That Jesus is the essential foundation of the church (1 Corinthians 3:11)
- That if the foundation is missing, the church has nothing to build upon (Luke 6:46–49)
- That self-death is the foundation for making discipleship a daily practice (Luke 9:23–24)
- That a healthy vision is believers building up one another in love in the church through the use of their spiritual gifts and evangelizing the community (Philippians 2:1–16)
- In a manner that will convert spectators into ministers (2 Timothy 2:15)
- How the church body can help new members feel at home (Romans 12:1–5)
- What a mature disciple-making church will look like (Acts 2:41–47)
- The basic functions of a healthy church (John 13:34–35; Galatians 6:2; Philippians 2:1–4; James 5:16)
- How to overcome major obstacles to becoming a disciple-making church and do it in love (Romans 12:9–21)

You must illustrate your preaching and teaching by sharing how other churches have made the Great Commission a daily practice for their people.

THE PASTOR-TEACHER AND PERSPECTIVE

When our Lord's Great Commission becomes a daily practice for your church, you will see some results internally and externally. For example, internally you will see:

- Church leadership is functioning in submission to the Lord and one another (Ephesians 5:21).
- Leaders are perceiving the people as wanting to grow.
- The governing body is demonstrating ownership of the vision for operating and perpetuating their ministry of discipleship and evangelism.
- The leadership base is expanding to accommodate the future.
- Middle management is in place, meaning each major area of ministry is led by a qualified person who is committed to it.

- Disciple-making principles are permeating the education-training ministries of the church (John 14:15; 2 Timothy 3:16–17).
- Family growth and development are taking place (Ephesians 5:21; 6:4).
- Outreach, including evangelism, is incorporated in all areas of discipling ministry in order to help people focus less on self and more on the needs of others.
- New believers are flowing into the church.
- An increasing variety of ministries are surfacing as spiritual gifts are released in maturing believers.
- Greater numbers of men are attending services.

Externally, you will see:

- The church is intentionally helping other churches disciple and evangelize.
- People are recognizing their own daily-life mission field.
- The missions budget is expanding for extending the kingdom.
- The community is experiencing economic development.
- The crime rate, drug use, and teen pregnancy are dropping.

CONCLUSION

If you have the faith, God has the power. If you will put your confidence in God, He will do it (1 Thessalonians 5:24), because God can. So let God do it.

REFERENCES

Hull, B. 1988. *The disciple making pastor.* Old Tappan, N.J.: Revell.

McGavran, D. A., and W. C. Arn. *Ten steps for church.* New York: Harper & Row.

Overview of a church-centered vision and plan for the Great Commission. 1994. ChurchLIFE. Orlando, Fla.: Campus Crusade for Christ.

Sargent, T. 1994. *The sacred anointing.* Wheaton, Ill.: Crossway Books.

Vines, J. 1989. *Exploring 1–2–3 John.* Neptune, N.J.: Loizeaux.

Winters, T. J. 1996. Personal communication.

LEE N. JUNE

The Deacons' Role

LEE N. JUNE is a professor at Michigan State University and currently serves as assistant provost for Academic Student Services and Multicultural Issues, and is vice president for Student Affairs and Services. He was director of a university counseling center for eight and a half years. Born and reared in Manning, South Carolina, Lee holds a bachelor of science degree from Tuskegee University, a master of education degree in counseling, a master of arts degree in clinical psychology, and a doctor of philosophy degree in clinical psychology from the University of Illinois (Champaign-Urbana). He did postgraduate study in psychology at Haverford College (1966–67) and was a special student during a sabbatical leave at the Duke University Divinity School (1981). He is editor of two books, *Men to Men: Perspectives of Sixteen African-American Christian Men* (Zondervan, 1996), and *The Black Family: Past, Present and Future* (Zondervan, 1991). A member of the New Mount Calvary Baptist Church (Lansing, Michigan), Lee is married to Shirley Spencer June, and they have two sons, Stephen and Brian.

CHAPTER 5

LEE N. JUNE

The Deacons' Role

Those who have served well gain an excellent standing and great assurance in their faith in Christ Jesus.

1 Timothy 3:13

INTRODUCTION

This chapter focuses on the historical role of deacons in evangelism and discipleship and outlines the current challenges and opportunities for the office. We will begin by reviewing the biblical origins of and qualifications for the office. Then we will discuss the role of deacons in the New Testament and in churches today and suggest how deacons can be systematically involved in evangelism and discipleship.

BIBLICAL ORIGINS

The first appearance of the English word *deacons* in the biblical canon is in Philippians 1:1. Though not mentioned by the name *deacons,* details and the circumstances surrounding what is believed to be the origin of the office are found in Acts 6:1–7:

> In those days when the number of disciples was increasing, the Grecian Jews among them complained against the Hebraic Jews because their widows were being overlooked in the daily distribution of food. So the Twelve gathered all the disciples together and said, "It would not be right for us to neglect the ministry of the word of God in order to wait on tables. Brothers, choose seven men from among you who are known to be full of the Spirit and wisdom. We will turn this responsibility over to them and will give our attention to prayer and the ministry of the word."

> This proposal pleased the whole group. They chose Stephen, a man full of faith and of the Holy Spirit; also Philip, Procorus, Nicanor, Timon, Parmenas, and Nicolas from Antioch, a convert to Judaism. They presented these men to the apostles, who prayed and laid their hands on them.
>
> So the word of God spread. The number of disciples in Jerusalem increased rapidly, and a large number of priests became obedient to the faith.

Other references to deacons can be found in 1 Timothy 3:8, 10, and 12.

The Greek word for deacon is *diakoneo,* and for deacons it is *diakonos*. According to Strong (1995), to be a *deacon* means to be an attendant; to wait upon menially or as a host, friend, or teacher; to minister unto, or serve. Vine (1981, p. 272) defines *deacon* as a word that "primarily denotes a servant, whether as doing servile work, or as an attendant rendering free service."

BIBLICAL QUALIFICATIONS

The qualifications for deacons are explicitly outlined in Scripture. In Acts 6, as noted earlier, we saw that they were to be full of the Spirit and wisdom. In 1 Timothy 3:1–13 characteristics of deacons are much like those of bishops.

> This is a true saying, If a man desire the office of a bishop, he desireth a good work. A bishop then must be blameless, the husband of one wife, vigilant, sober, of good behaviour, given to hospitality, apt to teach; Not given to wine, no striker, not greedy of filthy lucre; but patient, not a brawler, not covetous; One that ruleth well his own house, having his children in subjection with all gravity; (For if a man know not how to rule his own house, how shall he take care of the church of God?) Not a novice, lest being lifted up with pride he fall into the condemnation of the devil. Moreover he must have a good report of them which are without; lest he fall into reproach and the snare of the devil. Likewise must the deacons be grave, not double-tongued, not given to much wine, not greedy of filthy lucre; Holding the mystery of the faith in a pure conscience. And let these also first be proved; then let them use the office of a deacon, being found blameless. Even so must their wives be grave, not slanderers,

sober, faithful in all things. Let the deacons be the husbands of one wife, ruling their children and their own houses well. For they that have used the office of a deacon well purchase to themselves a good degree, and great boldness in the faith which is in Christ Jesus. (KJV)

Because of the critical importance of qualifications, I will discuss these in detail in a later section.

DEACONS' ROLE IN THE NEW TESTAMENT

Little is written about the actual activities of all seven of the original deacons. The exceptions, however, are the activities of Stephen and Philip. In Acts 6 the deacons collectively assumed the daily service of the tables so that no one was neglected and so that the apostles could give their attention "to prayer and the ministry of the word" (v. 4). What is extremely significant to note is the fourfold effect of the deacons' service on the overall development of the early church (see vv. 7–8):

1. The Word of God spread.
2. The number of disciples increased rapidly.
3. A large number of priests became obedient to the faith.
4. Stephen did great wonders and miracles among the people.

Stephen is presented in Acts 6 and 7 as speaking the Word of God before the Sanhedrin with wisdom and power. His listeners became so outraged with his message that they killed him.

Philip is seen in Acts 8 preaching Christ in a city in Samaria, where his preaching was accompanied by great signs and miracles (v. 13). He also evangelized and baptized the Ethiopian eunuch (vv. 26–39), an important official in charge of the treasury of Candace, queen of the Ethiopians, and preached in numerous other cities (v. 40). The final reference to Philip is in Acts 21:8, where he is described as an evangelist.

The individual activities of Procorus, Nicanor, Timon, Parmenas, and Nicolas are not presented. These five are only named in Acts 6:5. Nevertheless, the powerful fourfold effects of their collective efforts have been previously noted.

In summary, the activities of the deacons in the early church were:

- Waiting on tables (Acts 6:2)
- Doing great wonders and miracles (Acts 6:8)

- Speaking the Word of God before the Sanhedrin (Acts 7:2–53)
- Submitting to martyrdom (Acts 7:54–60)
- Preaching Christ in a city in Samaria (Acts 8:5)
- Evangelizing and making disciples (Acts 8:12)
- Conversing with and preaching to the Ethiopian eunuch (Acts 8:30–37)
- Baptizing the Ethiopian eunuch (Acts 8:38)
- Preaching in various other cities (Acts 8:40)

DEACONS TODAY: WHAT IS NEEDED

Are the original criteria for deacons still applicable? How should deacons be selected? What are to be their duties?

The answers to these questions vary by denomination and local church membership. I believe, however, that if deacons are to be effective and involved in evangelism and discipleship, they must be properly selected, properly trained in how to evangelize and disciple, and their work must be valued and reinforced in their local church.

Proper Selection

Proper selection is probably the most critical of the three factors. Deacons must be selected according to the biblical criteria of 1 Timothy 3:1–13 (see above). There must be no shortcuts made in hope that the person will eventually grow into the qualifications.

Deacons are to be readily recognized by their congregation as persons who have integrity and are spiritually mature ("full of the Spirit and wisdom," Acts 6:3). This was unquestionably the case with the deacons chosen in Acts 6. The result of selection on the basis of these qualifications profited the church greatly (the fourfold effect).

Now let us examine in detail the qualifications for deacons as listed in 1 Timothy 3.

Grave. The Greek word for "grave" is *semnos.* It means honorable or honest. Deacons are to be persons who have a solid reputation, integrity, and high moral character. (For a further discussion on the importance of moral character, see June 1996.)

Not double-tongued. The Greek word for "double-tongued" is *dilogos,* which means telling a different story. Deacons are to be truthful, not persons who tell different stories depending on the situation or audience.

Not given to much wine. Deacons are not to be regular drinkers of alcohol.

Not greedy of filthy lucre. The NIV translates the Greek here "not a lover of money." Deacons are not to covet money or to be vulnerable to seeking gain through deceitful means.

Holding the mystery of the faith in pure conscience. The Greek word for "mystery" is *mysterion,* which means secret. The Greek word for "pure" is *katharos,* which means clean or clear. And the Greek word for "conscience" is *suneidesis,* from the word *suneido,* which means to see completely or to understand. Thus, deacons are to hold precious the Word of God and have an understanding of it and its importance.

Proved. The Greek word for "proved" is *dokimazo,* which means to approve, examine, or try. Deacons are to have a track record of honesty and integrity in the faith before their selection. They must not be inexperienced in the faith.

Found blameless. The Greek word for "blameless" is *anegkletos,* which means unaccused or irreproachable. This characteristic goes with "proved." Deacons must be found to have a record of integrity and honesty.

Have wives who are ... The spouses of deacons are to be grave (i.e., honest), not slanderers (the Greek word is *diabolos,* which means false accuser), sober (the Greek word is *nephalios,* which means circumspect or vigilant), and faithful in all things.

Husbands of one wife. Deacons who are married are to be in a monogamous relationship.

Ruling their children and their own houses well. Deacons are to be in right relationship with their children and with their own households while exercising proper biblical oversight.

Proper Training

Proper training is the next important characteristic. If deacons are first properly selected, they will have already had some training and experiences in the faith. Proper training should entail, at least, grounding in the basics of Christianity, learning to clearly present the plan of salvation, and learning to disciple new converts.

Grounding in the basics of Christianity. The original deacons clearly had a good grasp of their faith. If they had not, they would not have been selected. The effective activities in which they later engaged give further evidence of their grounding in the faith.

Persons who are already deacons should make every effort to get additional training through whatever means are available in their local communities. They should also be taking advantage of training within the local church, including regularly attending Sunday school and Bible study in addition to personal Bible study.

Learning to clearly present the plan of salvation. The first deacons were able to clearly present the gospel so that persons would be led to make a decision to receive Christ. Philip's encounter with the Ethiopian eunuch is a vivid example of this ability.

For those who do not have a method of clearly presenting the plan of salvation, I recommend the tract *Have You Heard of the Four Spiritual Laws?* (Bright 1994). The four spiritual laws presented in this booklet are:

1. God loves you and offers a wonderful plan for your life (John 3:16; 10:10).
2. Man is sinful and separated from God. Thus he cannot know and experience God's love and plan for his life (Romans 3:23; 6:23).
3. Jesus Christ is God's only provision for man's sin. Through Him you can know and experience God's love and plan for your life (John 14:6; Romans 5:8; 1 Corinthians 15:3–6).
4. We must individually receive Jesus Christ as Savior and Lord; then we can know and experience God's love and plan for our lives (John 1:12; 3:1–8; Ephesians 2:8–9; Revelation 3:20).

This tract also contains some helpful diagrams, a prayer for salvation, and helps for growth in the Christian life.

Another salvation tract that is more geared toward the African-American community is *The Key to Life* (Ballard 1982). Its message and methodology are similar to *The Four Spiritual Laws.* Jesus Christ is presented as the perfect key, and as such, gives eternal life to those who receive Him.

Deacons should have at least one method of leading others to Christ with which they are comfortable. Various tracts can be found in any Christian bookstore. Deacons are encouraged to review these tracts and include the one of choice in their personal "tool kit." (For additional information on how to evangelize and disciple, see Richardson 1991.)

Learning how to disciple new converts. Evangelism and discipleship must go hand in hand. Deacons who do not know how to disciple a person should search for a seminar on discipling. Christian bookstores carry a variety of useful materials that can be studied and used as aids in discipling. One good resource is *The Discipleship Series: Eight Essentials for Spiritual Growth* (Scazzero 1992). The topics covered in the series are New Life in Christ, Basic Beliefs, Building Character, Spiritual Disciplines, Knowing Scripture, Sharing Your Faith, Spiritual Warfare, and Effective Prayer. Another example is the series *Design for Discipleship* (1980) published by NavPress. Seven topics are covered in this series: Your Life in Christ, The Spirit-Filled Christian, Walking with Christ, The Character of the Christian, Foundation for Faith, Growing in Discipleship, and Our Hope in Christ. This series come with a leader's guide.

Valuing and Reinforcing the Work of Deacons

The local church must value and reinforce the deacons' proper selection and work. If it doesn't, the deacons will spend most of their time doing nonessentials or tasks that may be important but have little or nothing to do with evangelism and discipleship.

It is unfortunate that the role of deacons is being deemphasized in many congregations. Maybe this is why, in some cases, we are not experiencing the fourfold effects of their service as experienced in the early church.

CHALLENGES TO DEACONS AND CHURCHES

For the body of Christ to function most effectively, we must understand that the entire membership has a vital function to carry out. While the Bible speaks of certain offices (bishop, pastor, deacons) and gifted people (apostles, prophets, evangelists, pastors, teachers), it is clear that these are designed for order and effectiveness, not superiority. The passage that follows the references to gifted persons reads:

> It was he who gave some to be apostles, some to be prophets, some to be evangelists, and some to be pastors and teachers, to prepare God's people for works of service, so that the body of Christ may be built up until we all reach unity in the faith and in the knowledge of

the Son of God and become mature, attaining to the whole measure of the fullness of Christ.

Then we will no longer be infants, tossed back and forth by the waves, and blown here and there by every wind of teaching and by the cunning and craftiness of men in their deceitful scheming. Instead, speaking the truth in love, we will in all things grow up into him who is the Head, that is, Christ. From him the whole body, joined and held together by every supporting ligament, grows and builds itself up in love, as each part does its work. (Ephesians 4:11–16)

The Bible declares that all members have gifts and that those gifts are given by the Holy Spirit. Therefore, all are expected to be involved in the work of the ministry.

CONCLUSION

This chapter has presented an overview of the historical origin of the office of deacon and has examined the early effectiveness of this office. I have suggested some evangelistic and discipleship tools and have discussed some contemporary challenges. It is my hope that the reader will make use of this material to the glory of God and His kingdom.

REFERENCES

Ballard, R. 1982. *The key to life.* Dayton: Home Ministries.

Bright, B. 1994. *Have you heard of the four spiritual laws?* Orlando: New Life.

Douglas, J. D. 1962. *The new Bible dictionary.* Grand Rapids: Eerdmans.

June, L. N. 1996. The importance of moral character. In *Men to men: Perspectives of sixteen African-American Christian men,* edited by L. N. June. Grand Rapids: Zondervan.

Navigators. 1980. *Design for discipleship.* Colorado Springs: NavPress.

Richardson, W. 1991. Evangelizing the Black male: Critical issues and how-to's. In *The Black family: Past, present and future,* edited by L. N. June. Grand Rapids: Zondervan.

Scazzero, P. 1992. *The discipleship series: Eight essentials for spiritual growth.* Grand Rapids: Zondervan.

Strong, J. 1995. *The new Strong's exhaustive concordance of the Bible.* Nashville: Thomas Nelson.

Vine, W. E. 1981. *Vine's expository dictionary of Old and New Testament words,* edited by F. F. Bruce. Old Tappan, N.J.: Revell.

PART THREE

Training Laborers for
Evangelism and Discipleship

ROLAND G. HARDY JR.

Christian Education: Making the Process Work

ROLAND G. HARDY JR. is the senior attorney in the law office of Roland G. Hardy, Jr. & Associates and has practiced in the Woodbury, New Jersey, area for more than twenty years. He is also the president-founder of Renaissance Productions, Inc., an African-American Christian publishing and distribution company in Woodbury, and president-founder of the Urban Family Network, a worldwide internet communication network designed to encourage Christian ministries, businesses, and individuals to collaborate in order to build strong Christian families in cities.

Hardy has served the local and national African-American community in various capacities, including co-chairman of the National Congress on the Urban Family in Atlanta in June 1997; board member of the Institute for Black Family Development in Detroit; former executive vice president of the Urban Alternative in Dallas; political action chairperson of the NAACP for the state of New Jersey; member of the White House Task Force on the Black Family in 1987; Gang Violence Task Force, Los Angeles County, in 1988; former board member of the Association of Trial Lawyers of America—New Jersey; and former president of the South Jersey Lawyers' Association.

Hardy received his undergraduate degree from the University of Delaware and a juris doctorate from the University of Santa Clara, California. He and his wife of 21 years, Delores, reside in Pitman, New Jersey, with their two children, Ayanna and Roland III. They fellowship at the Living Word Bible Fellowship in Blackwood, New Jersey.

CHAPTER 6

ROLAND G. HARDY JR.

Christian Education: Making the Process Work

On any Sunday morning in the African-American church community, just as in any other church community in America, you will find the ritual of Sunday school being conducted. Men, women, and children gather before the worship hour to learn about their faith by "going through the Sunday school lesson." Traditionally, this lesson time is limited to an hour and includes the mandatory opening hymn, prayer, and remarks by the Sunday school superintendent before the students assemble in their respective classes. Prior to dismissal, the offering is taken and the treasurer's report and student lesson summaries are given. The actual time devoted to teaching the lesson ends up being approximately twenty-five to thirty minutes, about enough time to read the lesson and review the memory verses. If by the time the superintendent rings the bell signaling time to take up the offering, a class has not completed the lesson, the teacher rushes through the balance of the lesson for completion's sake.

What is communicated when lessons are presented as described above? I suggest little more than disconnected Bible information in the name of content. Although Sunday school literature publishers make a valiant attempt to organize and design user-friendly, Bible-based curricula, the constraints of the traditional Sunday school format, coupled with the disconnected information, prevent students from gaining an understanding of the full counsel of God. Students experience difficulty connecting the historical significance of Bible stories and personalities to the advent of Jesus Christ and then to their present circumstances and individual journeys. This sense of disconnectedness is exaggerated by the "rush through" format.

Although the intent of the Sunday school lesson is to communicate Bible information in such a way as to bring students to an understanding of who God is and how He wants to relate to His creation, what is actually communicated is that tradition and ritual are much more important than a genuine understanding of and relationship with God. More often than not, students take away the thought that it is acceptable to offer God whatever type of service they can fit in.

Unfortunately, the concept of Christian education, for many churches, has become limited to the Sunday school ritual. In these churches, regretfully and unfortunately, there is no connection between Christian education and the development of young believers into mature saints.

THE CHRISTIAN EDUCATION MANDATE

The following New Testament Scriptures provide a biblical mandate for Christian education.

> Go and make disciples of all nations, baptizing them in the name of the Father and of the Son and of the Holy Spirit, and teaching them to obey everything I have commanded you. And surely I am with you always to the very end of the age. (Matthew 28:19–20)

> All Scripture is God-breathed and is useful for teaching, rebuking, correcting and training in righteousness, so that the man of God may be thoroughly equipped for every good work. (2 Timothy 3:16–17)

Christian education must be viewed in a broad sense and is the very process that undergirds the entire mission of the church. Unless a person knows God and God's commandments, expectations, and promises, that person will find it impossible to experience the fullness of God's plan. The overall educational process should be designed to equip believers with the knowledge and understanding necessary to develop into mature saints.

AVENUES FOR CHRISTIAN EDUCATION: MODE AND METHOD OF COMMUNICATION

Understanding that society's mode and method of communicating have changed drastically over the past ten years is a first step toward accomplishing the biblical Christian education mandate. We have moved from cordless to cellular phone, from single-image to multiple-image television, and from newspaper to Internet. Each advance has sped up the delivery of information and introduced a new way of communicating. Therefore, our expectations relative to the mode and method of information delivery have also changed. We have become accustomed to immediate access to information in the form of sound bites, icons, and headlines. Our attention span wanes after a brief period of time unless we are stimulated by visuals or theatrics. Despite these new forms of communication, the mode and method of communicating Bible information within most churches have not changed in over a hundred years. Is there any wonder that most churches have enormous difficulty attracting and keeping children and young adults?

WHAT CHRISTIAN EDUCATION MUST BECOME

If we are to fulfill our mandate to equip believers (make disciples), Christian education must be viewed as an intricate, indispensable, and ongoing process that touches every aspect of ministry. It must not be limited to one day nor one form of delivery. It must incorporate curricula, books, video, audio, drama, and other forms of communication as aids to understanding Scripture. It must contain interactive components to facilitate maximum internalization of the subject matter. Remember, the objective is to provide students with biblical information and a context for its application in their lives.

Using Age-Appropriate Materials

It is extremely important that age-appropriate, relevant resources be incorporated into the teaching of the church body. Age appropriateness refers to material content and form of presentation. Not only must the material be biblically accurate, it must also be engaging. The comprehension ability and attention span of a first grader is different than that of a sixth grader. Thus, what we teach and how we teach it will also differ.

Consider the various forms of communication that engage first graders: brightly colored picture books; high-energy, contemporary musical audio and video presentations; and character-driven story lines with a single theme, to name a few. The interchangeable use of these types of communication helps maintain children's interest. Obviously, sixth graders are able to handle more text-driven material but are probably acclimated to musical audio and video presentations as the communication form of choice. Sixth graders are much more interactive and therefore need discussion formats and exploration exercises.

Using Relevant Materials

Christian education materials must also be relevant; that is, they must address the circumstances and issues confronted by students. There are two types of relevance that are important to the spiritual development of African-American believers: cultural and developmental.

Unfortunately, most Christian education materials produced by traditional publishing houses are written from a middle-class, White, suburban perspective. Those publishing houses that have made an effort to address the broad relevancy issue, however, have done so with middle-class, White, suburban writers interpreting the African-American experience. It is absolutely essential that your Christian education material bring the truth of the gospel to the circumstances of the African-American experience in such a way as to promote historical inclusiveness and contemporary relevance.

It is well documented that our churches are losing African-American boys by the time they reach twelve years old. One reason for this loss is that we have not made the gospel relevant to them. The magnificence of the ministry of Jesus Christ is that He was able to relate the Word of God to the circumstances of the people to whom He was ministering. In John 4, when speaking with the Samaritan woman, Christ was able to relate His message to her cultural background. Further, in His parables He used life circumstances with which His audience was familiar. Christian education materials must bring the same type of realism to the gospel message.

In addition to being culturally relevant, materials must be developmentally relevant. There are at least six developmental stages in the life of a person: childhood, preadolescence, adolescence, young adulthood, middle-age, and elderhood. Each stage has its priorities and challenges. With children the focus is on exploration. The preadolescent years are highlighted by the quest for independence. The adolescent stage prioritizes individualism and relationship development with a constant fear of rejection. Young adults devote much of their thought life to career and finding the right mate. Middle-agers tend to reflect on their accomplishments and are challenged by the lure of youthfulness. The elderly have health issues as their top priority and are in the process of preparing for death. If we accept these stages as true, then our approach to Christian education must assign the same priorities, which must be reflected in our teaching. How frustrating it is for an adolescent struggling with the concept of dating and relationships to be constantly taught about death and going to heaven.

To ensure a balanced and effective biblical approach to Christian education, we must first redefine its role in the life of the church as the process of equipping believers with the tools necessary to attain spiritual maturity with the aid of the Holy Spirit. This process must be sensitive to the cultural and developmental needs of the audience and must utilize the appropriate methods of communication to reach them.

Resources

The following publishers have resources that may be of benefit to the church in fulfilling its Christian education mandate:

Creation House Publishers, 600 Rinehart Road, Lake Mary, FL 32746; (800) 283-8494; http:\\www.strang.com

Christian Research and Development, 27 West Township Line Road, Upper Darby, PA 19083; (800) 5511-CRD

Echoes (Division of Cook Communications), 4050 Lee Vance View, Colorado Springs, CO 80918; (800) 708-5550

Moody Press, 820 N. LaSalle Boulevard, Chicago, IL 60610; (312) 329-2101; http:\\www.moody.edu

Renaissance Productions, Inc., 537 Mantua Avenue, Woodbury, NJ 08096; (800) 234-2338; http:\\www.urbanfamily.com

Urban Ministries, Inc., 1557 Regency Court, Calumet, IL 60409; (773) 233-4499; http:\\www.urbanministries.com

Zondervan Publishing House, 5300 Patterson Avenue, S.E., Grand Rapids, MI 49530; (616) 698-6900; http:\\www.zondervan.com

CONCLUSION

This chapter is designed to encourage you to expand your thought process as it relates to Christian education. Christian education has been presented as a broad concept with a clear biblical mandate: We are commanded to make disciples by equipping the saints. In carrying out this mandate, we must keep a focus, use the various modes and methods of communication, and make use of culturally and developmentally appropriate materials. We can and must make the learning process exciting, challenging, and fun.

DAVID GOUGH

Youth: Doing It with Music

DAVID GOUGH grew up in Detroit, Michigan, and is the owner of DoRohn Records Company and Devmon Distributing Company. He attended the University of Guam and Henry Ford Community College. He is a songwriter, producer, musician, gospel singer, and businessperson. A member and deacon at the New Fellowship Tabernacle Church of God in Christ (Detroit), David is married to Carolyn Gough, and they have three sons, Damon, David, and Devin.

CHAPTER 7

DAVID GOUGH

Youth: Doing It with Music

INTRODUCTION

Today's youth experience and enjoy a variety of musical styles. Because music affects individuals in different ways, gospel music is very significant in evangelizing, particularly young people. The rap–hip-hop sound of today has given birth to a style that, in all honesty, has not been as fully embraced by the African-American church as it has by the White church. The White church has opened its doors to rap, rock gospel, and heavy metal gospel, which have reportedly been influential in hundreds of youth giving their lives to Christ. The African-American church, with its form of soul-stirring music that is rooted in Negro spirituals and anthems, has moved much more slowly toward accepting alternative contemporary styles of spreading the Good News in song.

With the dawning of a new millennium, we find ourselves being presented with gospel songs done in styles totally uninhibited by traditional restraints other than giving praise and honor to God. A modern gospel song may even be accompanied by a young woman and/or young man doing an interpretive dance, or a twenty-person step team (drill team, as we used to call them) shouting out Scripture as cadence and rhythmically marching in precise togetherness. From a gospel soloist, to praise bands, from interpretive dancers to the ever-loved gospel choir, gospel music is a force that can unquestionably be thought provoking and life changing, and should be taken throughout the world.

JAMMIN' FOR JESUS

"Did you hear how tight that track was?"

"That new CD was slammin'."

"This live recording is sweet."

These are some of the expressions that one may hear in an after-church conversation between two young people discussing some of the latest gospel music they've heard. Within the last decade gospel music has increased in popularity tenfold. Always a mainstay but considered secondary music, gospel music is not just for Sunday anymore. Tight instrumentation and slick lyrical content, along with a lot of substance, has caught the ears of people from ages eight to eighty.

The popularity of gospel music today has taken it to such social functions as roller-skating parties. I'm reminded of the first time I attended a gospel skating party. The evening started off with the D.J. asking everyone to stop moving while a word of prayer was given. This set the tone for the entire evening. The crowd of approximately eleven hundred people, ranging in age from eighteen to twenty-five, skated to the sounds of contemporary gospel music, pausing now and then for a snack and some conversation. Here and there I overheard pockets of witnessing to the goodness and saving power of Jesus Christ. The term "gospel skating party" was not a turnoff to anyone there, not even nonbelievers, for they left that evening wanting to know when the next party would be. As one parent put it, "There's no riff-raff here."

Another time I witnessed the effectiveness of gospel music was when I was on a concert tour in New Orleans performing with Kirk Franklin and the Williams Brothers in Louis Armstrong Park. The weather was extremely warm, but it did not deter the crowd from coming out to hear the name of Jesus being lifted up in song. Two-thirds of the crowd were young people, and every song was received with thunderous applause and the uplifting of hands in praise. During the altar call at this outdoor event, between fifty and a hundred young people gave their lives to Christ. This proves what God has said all along—that we are to go out to the roads and country lands and compel people with the Good News of Jesus Christ (Luke 14:23). Jesus said, "I, when I am lifted up from the earth, will draw all men to myself" (John 12:32).

LET THE MUSIC PLAY

There are individuals, choirs, and groups with music ministries who evangelize our youth in concerts across the country and around the world. The artist Carmen is one prime example of such a person; some of his concerts are staged with lights, fog machines, and theatrical splendor. Andrae Crouch is another effective musician who blazed a trail in contemporary Gospel for many of the well-known artists today. Fred

Hammond and Radical for Christ, Kirk Franklin and the Family, Hezekiah Walker and the Love Center Choir, John P. Kee and New Life, and God's Property are some of the Gospel groups today who have a heart beat for young people. Their music reflects the contemporary Gospel sound of our time.

Concerts often feature altar calls to youth that echo the message conveyed in the lyrics of many songs: that God is waiting to receive them because He loves them. Another theme presented in much of the music is that young people can be anything they want to be. Thus the music plants the seed in the fallow ground of the heart. Hundreds of youth have given their lives to Christ because they found expressed in the music feelings that they could relate to, and in the performers found people who could relate to them where they are.

Since musical styles vary and have proved to be so powerful with young people, they shouldn't be taken lightly and must always display the common thread of God's living Word and salvation.

GOD IS ALWAYS TALKING—WE'RE JUST NOT ALWAYS LISTENING

Over the last few years, I've learned that God is always talking but that we must have ears to hear. God has a definite heartbeat for young people, and if we will just apply ourselves to what moves God, we will have a fulfilled life. God tells us in His Word to give and it shall be given to us. By giving of my time and experience, not only am I gaining in return, but the spiritual gratification is unexplainable. You have nothing to lose and everything to gain by sharing. Sowing into our youth the positive elements and words that have gotten us where we are can only cause us to reap a harvest that will prove to be invaluable. Naturally, we're expected to nurture our own children and to want the very best for them. We must with the same compassion minister to youth outside our immediate families.

READ AND FOLLOW THE INSTRUCTIONS CAREFULLY

There is nothing that we can't do as God's people. God has provided everything we need to know and do in His prophetic Word. The Bible is the book of life, and in it are the issues of life. I have learned through the Word that we are to say what God says about a situation or circumstance and step out in faith knowing that God will perform that which He said He would do. Wanting to do for our youth is ordained of God. In other words, it is His will that we give to them, share with them, and sow into them.

DON'T STOP THE INERTIA

Because there was something I desired to do for youth, I went to God in prayer. I was immediately led to the fact that it was best to give of that which I had some knowledge. This is far less frustrating than trying to get a lot of people to come and help out with something I knew nothing about. I had faith that because I was doing God's will, He would send people to help.

I would like to share a key principle of the kingdom that will help you in every area of your life. Once I was in dire straits in my business. My distribution company was nearly shut down because of outside forces that wanted to destroy me. My supplier did not want to ship a very large order to my customer and had refused to do so for almost sixty days. If they didn't ship, I would lose my largest account and be in line for a possible lawsuit and ultimately the loss of my business.

To make a long story short, I was reminded by God through a friend that He was still in control. After having done all that I could do, I just stopped mentioning all the negative things that were coming against me and stood on God's Word by being patient and thanking Him for what He had done, as though it was already done. Just fifteen days before the deadline, God changed the supplier's no to yes. Praise God! Hebrews 11:1 says, "Now faith is being sure of what we hope for and certain of what we do not see." While doubt may enter your mind, you should never speak or succumb to it. Learn the language of silence (in other words, keep your mouth shut). If there is something you want for your youth group, or you just want to evangelize some lost young person(s), seek counsel from God, write the vision, speak what it is that you want to do. Then do what you said you were going to do and keep moving.

USING MUSIC TO EVANGELIZE

The spoken Word of God is the most important element in the church. The ministry of music can be used to enhance the overall ministry. It goes without saying that there is nothing more exciting on a Sunday morning than when the pastor and the musician are clicking. It draws on the fullness of listeners, including emotions, and causes a quickening of the spirit. What gospel music does inside the church, it can also do for an entire community.

If more and more churches would open their doors and minds and let youth groups have gospel music settings in their fellowship halls on an off-service night so as to express themselves through their diverse styles of gospel music, souls could be won for the kingdom and pews could be filled with more youth.

If you really want to be daring, set aside the fifth Sunday morning of each month, which occurs four times a year, and give it to the music department to conduct a youth rally with emphasis on artistic expression through gospel music. Upon getting your pastor's approval, you could distribute a flyer calling all who would want to express themselves artistically. Have the program open to gospel rappers, soloists, groups, mimes, and dancers. You can be sure to have an outpouring of enthusiastic young people who will be more than happy to share their gifts. And they will draw other young people.

TAKING IT TO THE STREETS

If the church does not have a fellowship hall, go and talk to the owner of the local deli or short-order restaurant and ask to use their facilities for one Sunday every other month just for starters. Possibly, the church and restaurant could partner. It may sound a little out of the norm, but that's exactly what we're talking about—tossing the net way out.

Some cities are having great success with this concept every Sunday. For example, Dulin's in Los Angeles, Sylvia's Soul Food in New Jersey, and The House of Blues in New Orleans, just to name a few. I've been told that the rewards have been great. If you want to get creative, put up a tent and have a gospel rap–hip-hop service with a youth minister in place for an altar call. When you really desire to do something with gospel music, God's list of roads and country lanes is vast.

PART FOUR

Practicing Evangelism and Discipleship at Home and at College

MICHAEL R. LYLES

Fatherhood: The Ultimate Head Coaching Job

MICHAEL R. LYLES is in private practice of psychiatry with Lyles & Crawford Clinical Consulting in Atlanta. Formerly he was the medical director of the Rapha Inpatient Adult Unit at Charter Peachford Hospital in Atlanta. He received his bachelor of science and doctor of medicine degrees from the University of Michigan and completed his psychiatric residency at Duke University. Michael is a member of the Zion Baptist Church in Roswell, Georgia, and is currently a Sunday school teacher. He also works with the children's church program. Born in Chicago, and raised in Spartanburg, South Carolina, he moved to Detroit as a teenager. He is married to Marsha Washington Lyles, and they have one son, Michael, and two daughters, Morgann and Mallory.

CHAPTER 8

Fatherhood: The Ultimate Head Coaching Job

My father and I are not close, and that bothers me. He would
shop with us as children, take us to games, and buy us candy.
However, we seldom talked about anything, and he rarely gave
me direction. It wasn't until I became a young adult that I real-
ized that something was missing. I needed more than food, shel-
ter, and entertainment from him. Now that I am a father, I find
myself repeating the same pattern.

Lee B.

Fatherhood is a difficult job for which few of us are prepared. Lee's uncertainty about his fathering is shared by many who had mixed experiences with their fathers. The uncertainty becomes nearly painful for those who were reared without a father to whom they could relate. Some fathers deny relationships with their children, as Lee's dad apparently did. Others deal with this void by denying their responsibility and abandoning their families.

Most men do not see fatherhood as an art or skill that has to be developed. As a youth, I spent my time trying to perfect my jump shot or hit a curve. My friends did not sit around and discuss how to become a good father and husband. We seldom discussed it at church. We spent far more time discussing how to "play" women like we played ball—not listen to, understand, or love women. Though I was fortunate to have a father in the home, we were not close and didn't discuss these kinds of issues either. Thus, my idea of a father centered around providing food, clothing, shelter, and entertainment—like Lee B.'s dad.

As I grew older, my interest in sports continued. I gave up the fantasy of ever being successful as a player but continued to be fascinated with the art of coaching. I read biographies of famous coaches and studied

109

their techniques, wishing that I could become one. After my conversion, God used that desire as he called me to "coach" a group of men in a college discipleship ministry. Later as a medical professional I had the opportunity to "manage" a team of health-care professionals for nearly a decade as a medical director. Like most men, I became obsessive about my work and became nearly as much a workaholic as the famous coaches whom I had studied. Any neglect of my family was justified by my need to provide for them.

However, God called me to leave that position and go in a very different direction. On my last day I sadly mused about how I would miss being a "head coach" of our medical team and felt like I was retiring. Then almost audibly God spoke to me. He said that He had called me to coach a team that I had neglected—my family. He reminded me, this old sports junkie, that I had three kids/players to coach and a very talented wife/assistant coach to nurture. He reminded me that I needed to make this a priority because I was accountable to Him for this responsibility (1 Timothy 3:4–5, 12).

I didn't know how to be that kind of father. God would have to teach me. Through the study of His Word and learning from other men in my life, the vision of fatherhood as the ultimate coaching job became clearer. God used what I understood—sports—to teach me about what I did not understand—fatherhood. Below I will illustrate the biblical parallels between fathering and coaching.

MEET THE OWNER (1 JOHN 3:2–3)

God calls us to fatherhood—but not because we are so great. Because He loves us so much, He sees the potential in us that we cannot see. It is His responsibility to help us become "like Him" in character and behavior. The owner of a football team once said that the coach's job is to coach the players, but the owner's job is to coach the coach. To become a good father/coach, we must first recognize and develop our relationship with our Lord and be open and obedient to His teaching in our lives.

SIGN YOUR CONTRACT (MATTHEW 19:4–6)

If we are to coach our family, we must make a commitment to them. We cannot negotiate with other teams—that is, with other women, our parents, or our friends. We are called to leave our other commitments and focus on our commitment to our family—for better and for worse, through winning and losing. That's what marriage is all about. We sign a lifetime contract and give our wives and children no-cut contracts. This kind of stability cannot be given through "shacking," for a "shacking" coach is always free to negotiate with other teams and may be gone tomorrow.

HAVE "LOVE FOR THE GAME" (JEREMIAH 20:9; 1 PETER 1:22; 4:8)

Family relationships are difficult. Conflicts occur on a "team," and the head coach/father has to help make peace. It is a tough job that is not often appreciated, so we have to have a passion for loving our families. In the hard times we will need Jeremiah's God-given "fire in my bones" and Peter's God-given "fervent love." We must really want to see our families succeed. A person with a passive, disinterested attitude need not apply for this job.

COACH YOUR ASSISTANT COACH (EPHESIANS 5:25, 33; 1 PETER 3:7)

One of the first things a successful coach does is hire good assistants. God gives us our wives to assist us in coaching our families. Smart head coaches recognize the strengths of their assistants and delegate appropriate authority to them. They also recognize their responsibility to build up, support, and nurture their assistants. Successful head coaches do not boss around their assistants. Successful fathers love, respect, and nurture their wives without being threatened by their talents. Instead, they learn how to work together as an administrative unit with their children. A famous coach once commented that he spent as much time coaching his coaches as he did his players, because the assistant coaches had more hands-on time with the players. Sounds like good advice to most of the husbands I know.

ESTABLISH YOUR PLAYBOOK (PSALM 119:9, 105; 2 TIMOTHY 3:14–17)

The identity of a team is influenced largely by its playbook. It is the responsibility of the father/head coach to establish the playbook—not the players or the assistant coaches. This is part of leadership. The Word of God is the playbook for a successful Christian family. Anyone who does not know the plays will be prone to error. Do your children have their own Bible in a form they can understand? Do they have appropriate resources to help them study it? Are you exposing them to Bible study opportunities that will deepen their understanding of the Word?

GET TO KNOW YOUR PLAYERS WHERE THEY ARE (PSALM 139:1–4; ROMANS 15:7)

A certain football coach was famous for knowing his players by number, not name. In time his players grew to resent this, and the team declined for a number of reasons. Scripture teaches us that God knows us very intimately, the way we are—not the way He wants us to be. God accepts us where we are and grows us into "new creatures." A good father takes the time to get to know his family very well, the way they are now, not the way he wants them to become. Our families need to feel loved and accepted before they can feel free to grow.

IDENTIFY AND DEVELOP THEIR GIFTS (ROMANS 12:3–8; 1 CORINTHIANS 12:12–31)

A high school football coach was deemed a genius when he converted a sophomore defensive back into a tailback who won all-American honors as a senior. In response, the coach pointed out that it took him one and a half years to realize that the player was at the wrong position. Our children are all different. It is our job to help them identify and grow their talents and gifts. To do this, we must spend time getting to know them and nurturing them. They must trust us enough to show us their best. This is where edifying their strengths is far more important than focusing on their weaknesses.

TEACH, TEACH, TEACH (DEUTERONOMY 6:4–9; PROVERBS 1:8; 3:1–2; 4:1–4, 20–22)

Children need specific teaching on issues. Great coaches are known for their ability to motivate and teach, and great fathers must take responsibility for teaching their children and providing them with educational opportunities about life issues. I often ask men whom I respect about how they do devotions and Bible study with their families, for coaches must learn from one another (1 Peter 5:5). A friend encouraged me to become a teacher at my church so that I could influence my children's spiritual development. That was a good "coaching tip."

DEVELOP YOUR COACHING STYLE (EPHESIANS 6:4; COLOSSIANS 3:19–21)

Some coaches believe that fear and intimidation are the best motivators. I cannot find biblical support for that position. Instead, the Bible is clear that fathers are not to be abusive to their children. Rather, respect and trust must be gained through consistent living and fair behavior toward spouse and children. A good coach can get his players and staff to "buy into" what he is trying to do if it is presented properly and has merit.

DEVELOP DISCIPLINE (PROVERBS 29:17; HEBREWS 12:10–11)

As leader of the family, a father is responsible for setting the tone of discipline. It must be timely (Proverbs 29:15) and fair (Proverbs 29:17). It should not become excessive (Deuteronomy 25:1–3), but must be clear with a corrective point delivered in love (Hebrews 12:7–11).

EAT YOUR WHEATIES (TITUS 1:6–8)

Coaches teach in word and deed. A coach can never say, "Do as I say—not as I do." Players will do as you do before they do as you say. Fathers must practice good spiritual "work habits" as an example to their families. However, we must eat our spiritual "Wheaties" in order to have the character and behavior that God desires—whether our families are looking or not.

DEVELOP YOUR PLAYERS, NOT YOUR EGO (MATTHEW 20:25–28)

Jesus defined greatness in terms of service. A good father will be focused on developing his family, not on drawing attention to himself. After a recent Super Bowl game, a player commented that the coaches received so much attention that you would have thought they were playing. Our long-term job is to help our families become more Christ-like, for in the eyes of God, this is what winning is about.

DEVELOP FUTURE COACHES (2 TIMOTHY 2:2)

The ultimate measure of a coach's success is his ability to develop future successful coaches. As a father, my goal is that my kids will grow up with a clear view of what it means to be a parent so that they will select their spouses carefully and coach our grandchildren well. The easy part is that they can all use the same playbook.

TWO-MINUTE WARNING (2 TIMOTHY 3:10–11, 14–15)

Fatherhood is a difficult job. Our task is not to order our kids around. We cannot make them change into duplicates of ourselves, for we cannot make them into something they are not. Nor should we use them to get our needs met. Our task is to love them unconditionally and to teach and motivate. We need to build them up and give them a sense of vision. We must build relationships with our children, as Paul did with Timothy. This is necessary so that they will know us and our teaching of the Word in word and deed. A good father, like a good coach, cannot make his family win spiritually, but is responsible to the owner—God—for providing the proper teaching example and encouragement toward godliness (1 Peter 5:1–4).

For many of us, it is "late in the game." We have mismanaged our responsibilities and functioned as poor role models. However, it is never too late to trust God to help us do the right thing. We can begin to build bridges toward healthy relationships with our wives and children. We can begin to take responsibility for feeding them emotionally and spiritually, not just physically. We can become role models of righteousness so that our children feel free to imitate us as we follow and imitate Christ (1 Corinthians 4:4–16). These are difficult times for families. Young people desperately need leadership and love. With our playbook, the Word, in hand, it is time for us to get busy. If we do this, we will have been successful in presenting Christ to our families and discipling them.

RECRUITING (MATTHEW 28:19–20)

Many men cannot think of themselves as being good fathers because of poor relationships with their fathers. Others feel insecure about fatherhood due to the absence of a father or fathering role models. Some are afraid of taking the responsibility of fatherhood due to abusive relationships with alcoholic, drug-abusing, or womanizing fathers. All of these men need to know how God can make us into new creatures. The apple does not have to fall near the tree of our families of origin. When we truly "meet our owner," He can change us into something totally different with a power to live a righteous lifestyle.

However, most men are not aware that they can have a real relationship with God. As one rap artist said, when you grow up in the ghetto, that's all you know. Many of us grew up around so much "losing" in our families that we don't know anything else. That's why evangelism is important. Men without hope or a vision for successful family living have to be recruited to God's more excellent way. Woman and children without hope and vision need to be told of the God who will be a father to the fatherless (Psalm 68:5–6), a parent to the neglected (Psalm 27:10), and quite simply the best friend that anyone could ever have. This message has to be communicated by those who have experienced this relationship, for people without hope are interested in walk, not just talk. If we define winning as helping as many people as possible to become like Christ, recruiting will be an important aspect of our job as coach.

REFERENCES

Lewis, P. 1994. *The five habits of smart dads.* Grand Rapids: Zondervan.

McCartney, B. 1992. *What makes a man.* Colorado Springs: NavPress.

McClung, F. 1994. *God's man in the family.* Eugene, Ore.: Harvest House.

NORVELLA CARTER

Wives and Mothers:
Key Players in Evangelism and Discipling

NORVELLA CARTER is associate professor of education at Texas A & M University. She was born in Detroit and raised in Inkster, Michigan. She received a bachelor of science degree in special education and a master's degree in administration and supervision from Wayne State University in Detroit. She also received a doctor of philosophy degree from the Graduate School of Arts and Sciences at Loyola University of Chicago. She resides in College Station, Texas, with her husband, William Charles Carter Sr. They have seven children: Tracie, Camille, China, Crystal, William Jr., Kellie, and Victoria. Norvella is a member of St. John AME Church in Brenham, Texas. She is a couples ministry director along with her husband, and she serves on the board of directors of the Johnson-Ferguson Christian Academy that was founded by her church.

CHAPTER 9

NORVELLA CARTER

Wives and Mothers:
Key Players in Evangelism and Discipling

Although it was almost twenty-five years ago, it seems like yesterday that I was standing in front of the minister with my soon-to-be husband, getting ready to recite my marriage vows. We were in the upper level of a church, in a small office that had a love seat and a desk covered with books and papers. The minister wore a beautiful robe because he was going to the main sanctuary to officiate at a formal wedding after he married us. My girlfriend stood beside me, smiling and excited to be maid of honor. My groom was beaming, and his brother stood next to him with the ring.

Suddenly I began to reflect on the thought of becoming a wife in a few, short minutes, and my knees began to shake. Why was I being affected this way? Certainly we were in love and had talked about the details of marriage in depth. We were both Christians, independent, in our mid-twenties, and ready for marriage. Were these good reasons to get married? As my mind pondered these questions, my emotions soared out of control; and just as we began the short ceremony, I excused myself and ran to the bathroom located inside the small office.

As I shut the door, I dropped to my knees with excruciating stomach pain and began to pray that I would make a good wife. My mind began to race: *Why was I so nervous?. . .Why didn't we go to premarital counseling?. . .Maybe we should have had a wedding and told everyone we were getting married, including our parents. . . .Could we really get along?. . .Would we stay married?* I stayed in the bathroom so long that everyone was getting nervous and my girlfriend came in to see what was happening. She assured me that I was making the right decision and would live happily ever after if I could just straighten up and get through the ceremony.

My husband and I look back on the day we eloped and laugh at our naiveté. Unfortunately, I am not alone. Many women still enter into their role as wife without the slightest idea of what to expect. Many go into their role without the benefit of spiritual counseling, without intensive prayer for God's will, and without the knowledge of their power and responsibility within the marriage. This cycle usually continues as women become mothers and simply do as their mothers did without studying God's principles for successful mothering. The wife and mother who have not had the benefit of biblical training repeat this cycle from generation to generation. I, for example, had the benefit of a godly mother and mother-in-law, but I simply did not listen to their voices. I wish I had known that training takes time and that often it can take godly women several years to figure out that God designed the role of wife and mother as one of power, influence, and awesome responsibility.

As we focus on the twenty-first century, it is frightening to see the increases in African-American women who lack preparation as they enter marriage and motherhood. Marriages and families are under extreme attack. Statisticians predict that within the next decade one out of every two marriages will end in divorce and that the majority of children will live in broken homes (Wineberg 1990). There are various societal reasons for lack of preparation, such as increased mobility that cuts off interaction with the extended family; the breakdown of the family through death, divorce, and incarceration; increased work schedules outside the home for both parents; and the effects of poverty.

The African-American church can play a vital role in preparing young women for the future through evangelism and discipleship. The term *evangelism* means to share the gospel with others and tell them how to accept Jesus Christ as their personal Savior. The term *discipleship* puts an emphasis on teaching the Word of God to others and helping them to apply its principles to their lives. If spiritually mature wives and mothers in the church will take on the role of evangelizing and discipling younger wives and mothers, the church can reverse many of the social ills that are plaguing our communities and our country.

The purpose of this chapter is to encourage African-American wives and mothers (1) to recognize God's esteem for their roles, (2) to review a scriptural model that describes the role of a good wife and mother, (3) to recognize that mature Christian wives and mothers can be instrumental in evangelizing and discipling their younger counterparts, and

(4) to reflect on their personal stories of victory as disciplers and recipients of discipleship.

As we recognize and accept the wife and mother's role in evangelizing and discipling, we will be able to see how God saves marriages and preserves families. Older women who evangelize and disciple younger wives and mothers contribute to the stability of the family, add to the church, and carry out the commands of discipleship set forth in Scripture. When we look at the gruesome statistics that plague our people, we know and understand how vital this component is for the African-American family, church, and community.

GOD'S ESTEEM FOR THE ROLES OF WIFE AND MOTHER

It is amazing to see the way society treats two of the most vital roles on earth—those of wives and mothers. As African-American wives and mothers, we are part of the cornerstone of this nation. We are key players in society, yet evidence of our significance is not featured with the billboard proportions that other positions enjoy. Travel to your neighborhood bookstore and you will discover that books offering support specifically for Christian African-American wives and mothers are extremely scarce. Gratefully, the Lord in His Word designed a role for the wife and mother that gives us guidance, direction, and encouragement.

We are highly esteemed in God's eyes, which means that we are prized and respected by Him. We can see evidence of this esteem as our history begins, with the African, Edenic wife and mother in the Garden of Eden (Hilliard 1992; McKissic and Evans 1994; Williams 1994). Based on the biblical record, human origins began in Africa (Genesis 2:8–14), and throughout Scripture God reveals insight through wives and mothers of color such as Eve (Genesis 2), Ruth (Ruth), Bathsheba (2 Samuel 11:3–27), the wife of Joseph (Genesis 41:45), the wife of Moses (Numbers 12:1), and many others (June 1996).

As wives, God has given us a position of power that is unsurpassed in the life of our husbands. We are equal partners in marriage, and God has required the wife to come first with her husband, above his own mother and father. Our influence on our husbands is second only to God's. God will often use the wife to speak to the husband because she is close to his heart. We also know that our role as wives is highly esteemed by God, because His Word says that we are to be loved by our husbands to the point that they would die for us, even as Christ died for the church (Ephesians 5:25). We are very important.

God has given us, as wives and mothers, the charge of managing the family unit. All of society depends on a healthy, functional family unit. The wife and mother has the power to set the tone and climate of the home and to make it a place of refuge and protection for her husband and children. God has put our children's care, training, and spiritual upbringing into our hands. Our children will be the future citizens and leaders of society, and they are directly influenced by us. Our power and influence are far-reaching, as one can see, for example, when a child falls into sin and must stand before a judge. The judge will look into the background of that child to determine if he or she comes from a good home. Coming from a good home can enable a rebellious child to receive mercy from a judge. We should not underestimate the role God has given us as mothers. The values that we teach our children will carry on from generation to generation. The power that God has given to us is unique and unmatched on the earth. God holds our roles in high esteem.

THE ROLE OF A GOOD WIFE AND MOTHER

The role of a good wife and mother has been set forth in the Word of God through various models. This is important because these models identify the attributes and characteristics that we are to possess if we are going to be successful in our roles. In Proverbs 31:10–31, we can see a model of what God says is an ideal wife and mother. The following are a few points that should encourage you to do an in-depth study of this passage. Remember, these attributes are more reflective of an attitude than a specific action.

She fears the Lord (v. 30). This wife and mother is saved and has put the Lord at the center of her life. It is foolish to think that you can have a successful marriage and family life without the Lord. Women must receive the Lord Jesus Christ as their personal Savior before they can make the first step toward becoming a good wife and mother. This is why evangelism is such an important component of the African-American church. Wives, mothers, and all of humankind are hopeless until they become followers of Jesus Christ. Proverbs 1:7 says, "The fear of the LORD is the beginning of knowledge."

She is noble (v. 10). The term *noble* is defined as having high moral character, courage, generosity, and honor. This is significant, because the Scripture goes on to say that a woman of noble character is more valuable than precious stones and so trustworthy that her husband has complete confidence in her. This is the type of wife and mother who can provide stability within the home during times of trouble and crisis.

She speaks wisdom, and faithful instruction is on her tongue (v. 26). This wife and mother is spiritually mature, as evidenced by her ability to provide wisdom and instruction. She studies God's Word and is able to disciple others. She makes it her responsibility to avoid being ignorant and naive through personal growth and development. She is intelligent, wise, and educated. She gives appropriate counsel and watches what she says to others. As African-American wives and mothers, we should seek to acquire these attributes and begin to impact our families and communities.

She watches over the affairs of her household (v. 27). This wife and mother understands and values her position as a homemaker. She is faithful in managing her household well and does not view a job or outside position as more worthy than her own home life. As we live in a nation that has made materialism a god, we must not fall prey to the applause and secular rewards that require us to put our jobs first in our lives and in our hearts. Our history in this country has required most of us to work outside the home. That is not a problem unless the job causes us to neglect the affairs of our household. If you work outside the home, seek a position that will allow you to maintain the health and stability of your household.

She is not idle (v. 27). This wife and mother is productive and does not allow herself to be idle. Idle minds are open prey for the enemy. If you do not work outside the home, you have an opportunity to plan your life with more flexibility and have the potential to be more productive than the outside working wife and mother, especially in the home and church. This woman's activities enhance the household and gain respect from the community. Verse 15 says this wife and mother gets up early in preparation for a busy day.

She sets about her work vigorously; her arms are strong for her tasks (v. 17). This wife and mother has a healthy work ethic. She is not sluggish, overweight, or lazy. It is obvious that she works out and can go about her tasks with energy to spare. Many wives and mothers do care for their physical bodies with zeal. Too often, we as African-American women suffer from obesity, which causes high blood pressure, sugar diabetes, and an array of other ailments that are caused by poor eating habits. The Proverbs 31 wife and mother is an excellent model of one who takes care of her body and is not afraid to work on behalf of her household.

She opens her arms to the poor and extends her hands to the needy (v. 20). This wife and mother has compassion for those in poverty. She does not stop there, however; she actively seeks to relieve the suffering of the poor. As African-Americans, we have a disproportionate number of our people who live in poverty. A good wife and mother gives to the poor. She also supports and/or participates in programs that reduce human suffering.

She takes time to dress herself well and look good (v. 22). This wife and mother pays attention to her appearance. She is pleasing to the eyes of her husband, children, and those around her, but most of all, she dresses in a manner that pleases God. Remember, she has wisdom, and her appearance reflects that fact.

She has a mind for business and it benefits her home (vv. 16, 24). This wife and mother is able to make investments and earn a profit. If we study our heritage, we will find that many of our female African ancestors were shrewd businesswomen. They managed complex households and were able to earn profits and make investments from their household budgets.

This model of the ideal wife and mother has been set forth in Scripture so that we can clearly see how a good wife and mother looks. I suggest that you study Proverbs 31:10–31 and other models in the Bible thoroughly. Allow the Holy Spirit to teach you what God wants you to know as a wife and mother. Then begin to apply those principles to your life.

EVANGELIZING AND DISCIPLING: INSTRUMENTAL FOR AFRICAN-AMERICAN WIVES AND MOTHERS

Wives and mothers who manage their marriages, families, and households poorly are reaching epidemic proportions. The breakdown of the family is at an all-time high for African-Americans and has been attributed to every social ill imaginable (Santrock 1996). The African-American church is one of the first institutions to seriously address the issue of restoring marriages and families in the Black community. It is the only institution that proclaims Jesus Christ as the answer to home and community problems and seeks to address these problems at the heart of the issue, namely, through our reconciliation to God.

It is time for the church to take a greater role in bringing the Word of God to wives and mothers who are not saved and to begin discipling those who need to grow into mature Christians. All of us are to be evangelists and lead others to the saving grace of Jesus Christ. As Christians, evangelizing should be part of our lifestyle. The following are suggestions for Christian women who want to reach wives and mothers:

- Take a class or seminar that teaches you how to lead someone to Christ.
- Look for an opportunity to share the gospel with an unsaved wife and/or mother.
- Develop your testimony of faith, a long and short version, and share it when appropriate.
- Invite her to go to a Bible study, church service, or church social activity with you.
- Develop a friendship with her and allow her to view a Christian lifestyle.
- Begin to pray for her spouse and/or family.

Take advantage of classes that show videos, supply reading materials, conduct role-playing exercises, and allow you to observe home visitations with veterans who can answer your questions. Evangelism is the first step in the process of transforming women into godly wives and mothers who will impact the home, church, and the community.

We must recognize that mature Christian wives and mothers can be instrumental in discipling their younger counterparts. The term *discipleship* puts an emphasis on teaching the Word of God to others and helping them to apply the principles of Christian living to their lives. Discipleship usually takes place for a set period of time and may be conducted in a group session or one on one. In can be conducted in a range of forms and formats:

Bible studies
Classes
Seminars
Counseling
Retreats

Workshops
Social activities and outings
Home visitations
Trips, cruises
Small-group fellowships
Prayer breakfasts
Modeling through example

You may be led to disciple wives and mothers who are younger than yourself. Sheila Staley (1996, p. 75) writes that "visible groups of older women are desperately needed to influence the lives of younger women in the church today [because] the conditions of our homes, communities and work require women who understand God's principles for holy living." It takes time for women to understand and practice living a holy lifestyle.

Another reason for older wives to disciple younger wives deals with the issue of experience. Older wives have experienced the various phases of marriage and can relate to many situations that occur. The term "phases of marriage" can be defined as a specific time period in which certain events, issues, adjustments, and needs are typical and clearly different from those associated with other periods of the marriage (Rainey and Lewis 1993, p. 71). For example, a wife who is a newlywed would not face the same challenges as a wife who has been married for ten or twenty years.

Finally, you can witness to and encourage others anytime during your Christian experience, but if you are going to disciple others, you cannot be a novice. You must be a mature Christian who has demonstrated experiences of faith and depth with God. How is this faith and maturity developed? Scripture says that it is developed through suffering and trials of many kinds:

[We] rejoice in our sufferings, because we know that suffering produces perseverance; perseverance, character; and character, hope. And hope does not disappoint us, because God has poured out his love into our hearts by the Holy Spirit, whom he has given us. (Romans 5:3–5)

Consider it pure joy, my brothers, whenever you face trials of many kinds, because you know that the testing of your faith develops perseverance. Perseverance must finish its work so that you may be mature and complete, not lacking anything. (James 1:2–4)

It takes time to develop great faith and maturity. Older women have been given time and opportunities to grow. The apostle Paul says that older women should train the younger women and tells us where to get started in the discipling process. Titus 2:3–5 says:

> Teach the older women to be reverent in the way they live, not to be slanderers or addicted to much wine, but to teach what is good. Then they can train the younger women to love their husbands and children, to be self-controlled and pure, to be busy at home, to be kind, and to be subject to their husbands, so that no one will malign the word of God.

Older women who recognize and accept the role of evangelizing and discipling younger wives and mothers contribute to the stability of the family, add to the church, and carry out the commands of discipleship set forth in Scripture. Let us consider the training model that Paul writes about in Titus 2:3–5. He says that as wives and mothers, we should be trained in seven areas.

TO LOVE OUR HUSBAND

A young wife may be married for a few weeks or a few months before she realizes that loving her husband is not as easy and natural as she thought it would be before the wedding. It would be great if newly married couples could receive discipling through newlywed classes, marriage seminars, or counseling before the realization hits that all is not perfect.

I remember being invited to a weeklong Christian marriage seminar after I had been married for about eight months. Bill and I made plans to go, but his job sent him out of town. I decided not to go either, because I felt that he was the one who really needed it. Two years later we were invited again. Bill's schedule did not permit him to go, but I decided that I would go and get information to share with him. After all, he was the one who was making all the mistakes, and I wanted to help him.

The seminar was six to eight hours per day over a four-day weekend. The sessions were excellent and very comprehensive. After the four days, Bill inquired about the seminar, wanting to know if I enjoyed it. I was very quiet. How could I tell him that I learned I was selfish, unforgiving, judgmental, and unloving and that I held grudges? I was so convicted that it took months before I could share some of my experiences. A genuine transformation began to take place in me as I related to my marriage. I repented and asked the Lord to help me become a better wife. I also began to study the materials and with thoughtful purpose began to practice new behaviors.

My husband said it felt like he had a new wife. He began telling people that they should attend a marriage seminar before he had attended one himself. I remember him telling a friend, "Just send your wife if you can't go....You won't regret it." Since that time, we have attended many marriage classes, seminars, retreats, and training sessions. For the past few years, we have been counseling Christian couples through the church and working with Christian couples in small fellowship groups. Join a class or fellowship group; you will not regret it.

TO BE SUBJECT TO OUR HUSBAND

Paul's statement about subjection is a thorn to many new wives, but it is the role of the wife to be subject to her husband. Many wives do not know they have a serious problem in this area until after the marriage. God has given the husband the position of being the leader of the household, so the wife must respect the husband's position whether he is right, wrong, saved, or not saved. The role of older wives discipling younger wives is crucial in this area. Our behavior should be based on the Word of God and not on what we think, nor on what is traditional. I urge you to reflect on your role as a wife and engage in the following as you deepen your personal relationship with God and work toward strengthening your marriage:

- Pray for your marriage daily and ask God to help you stay in His will.
- Study the Word daily and seek wisdom from Scriptures that will strengthen your faith and that apply specifically to your role as a wife.
- Go to Christian classes, seminars, and retreats specifically designed for wives.
- Fellowship with other Christian wives and couples who have strong marriages.

Regretfully, we live in a time that requires me to add words for wives who are in abusive marriages. Seek Christian counseling immediately, and seek safety immediately if you or your children are in a life-threatening, abusive situation. Request help from your pastor and church leaders.

TO LOVE OUR CHILDREN

When I was a young wife and new mother, I had no idea that I would become the mother of seven children. Each child has been a milestone in my life. I love and adore each one, all of whom are special in their own way. My newborns helped me to understand the type of love that God has for His children, the type of love that says I will die for you. When they are tiny and totally dependent on you as a mother, you can see in them a parallel to your dependency on the Lord. We can do nothing without God (John 15:5).

Genesis 44:27–31 describes my relationship with each child as he or she was born. In this passage Judah makes a plea to Joseph and talks about the bond between Jacob and Benjamin. Judah says that his father's life is "closely bound up with the boy's life." I could not truly express my feelings about my children until I read this Scripture, but now I understand the relationship because I am "closely bound up" in their lives. The Lord gives us this type of love relationship so that we will have passion for evangelizing and discipling our children. Love gives us the zeal for making sure they have the protection of the Lord throughout their lives and into eternity. It is this love that enables us to embrace our role as mothers who evangelize and disciple our children. Later, as I grew in the Lord and studied the Scriptures, I also discovered that God gives us this type of love so that we can disciple other mothers and model this love before the world.

There was a time when I foolishly thought that all mothers loved their children because it was natural to all women. Those were times when abortion was illegal and people in general did not know the term "child abuse." Those were times when most mothers taught their daughters to love, cherish, and care for children. Those times are gone, and anyone who can read a newspaper knows that women do not naturally love their children. Anyone who can comprehend a radio or television news report that describes mothers who leave their newborns in garbage dumpsters and starve their young children knows that mothers do not have natural mothering instincts. Loving our children is something that is learned.

This message was made even clearer to me when I conducted research in what are called Child Parent Centers in Chicago schools. In these centers, parents of young children take parenting classes, and trainers teach each mother "skills" such as hugging and kissing their child, holding their child close, talking in a soothing voice, and reading to their child. Students also receive instruction in nutrition, housekeeping, and dressing their children in various seasons. Many areas need Child Parent Centers but do not have the funds. What happens to the mothers in those areas? The centers that exist are doing a fine job with the mechanics, but what about the spiritual needs of the mothers? It is evident that discipling can play a powerful role in the lives of mothers. Therefore, it is time for good mothers to begin to take on the role of evangelizing and discipling mothers in the church and community.

TO BE BUSY AT HOME

Many wives and mothers need discipling because they do not focus on their home as the base of operation—the place where families worship, plan, eat, sleep, study, love, nurture, wash, clean, play, entertain, relax, and retreat from the world. I am sure you can add to the list of activities that take place at your home. Paul says that we are to be busy at home. How do you know when a wife and mother is busy at home? There are many ways to know. It is apparent, for example, when you can look at her children and immediately detect that they are well cared for by the way they look, act, dress, and smell. The children of mothers who are overwhelmed by poverty are most likely to show neglect.

Churches need to play a greater role in helping the poor. They should set the pace in the community in assisting people to obtain the necessities for physical survival. Discipleship at this level means helping to meet physical needs, such as food, clothing, housing, furniture, and even employment. Jesus Himself fed hungry people and cared for their physical needs as a form of discipling. When we assist wives and mothers in this fashion, they readily receive the gospel and the principles of godly living. At that point, we can go into their homes and teach them how to cook, clean, study the Word of God, and be busy at home. I know this form of discipleship works, because I have seen churches that have food, clothing, housing, and furniture ministries. Some churches also assist people in finding employment. Through these churches we can see the lives of men and women who were in poverty transformed. These same individuals become active members of the church, testify of the Lord's goodness, and begin to help others change their lives.

Many other wives and mothers are not in poverty but need discipling because they do not focus on their home as their base of operation. Some other reasons a wife and/or mother is not busy in the home are:

- Her job or profession is more important than the home.
- She talks without limits, gossiping and slandering others.
- She drinks or engages in other substance abuse.
- She "acts single," meaning that she engages in excessive social activities outside the home.
- She watches television excessively—multiple soap operas, talk shows, videos, etc.
- She wants to be an evangelist and is away from the home often, yet her husband and children are not saved and do not go to church.

Certainly this list could go on. The home is the place where God houses the most important socialization unit on earth, the family. It is not difficult to see that older, godly wives and mothers can be instrumental in discipling their younger counterparts to be busy at home.

TO BE KIND

When my son William was born, it was one of the happiest days of my life. My husband, Bill, and I had four beautiful daughters, and the birth of a son was a joy to everyone in the household. Our girls had been very healthy, and it never occurred to us that anything could go wrong with our only son. We did not know it at the time, but eleven months later we found out that William had sickle-cell anemia, a blood disease that would change our lives forever. Sickle-cell anemia is an incurable disease of the red blood cells, and those who have it experience a great deal of pain, are susceptible to infections, and get tired easily. They also have what doctors call a "shortened life."

One day when William was in Children's Hospital in Detroit and was very sick with pneumonia and a collapsed lung, I had an unusual experience that demonstrated kindness beyond my belief. William was twelve months old at the time, and I was in the parents' lounge in the hospital praying fervently. It was about midnight, and I began to cry because doctors had said that it might be difficult for William to live to be three years old. I became hysterical and was on my knees weeping before the Lord. I was crying loud and saying over and over, "My son, my son, my only son; God have mercy. . . ." All of a sudden, an older African-American woman custodian, pushing a big cart with mops and towels, came into the lounge and said, "Baby, what's the matter? What's wrong?" In my hysteria, I could hardly talk. All I could say was, "My son, my son, my only son," over and over again.

The woman got one of the towels from her cart, soaked it in cool water, and wiped my face. She held me in her arms and began to talk to me. She asked me if I believed in Jesus as the Son of God and Savior of the world. I said yes and felt embarrassed because I loved the Lord, but it was not visible in my hysterical state. I managed to tell her that my son had sickle-cell anemia and was very ill in a room down the hall. She said, "Don't you know there are worse things in this world than sickle cell?" She told me that she knew all about "sicklers" because she had a child with sickle cell. She said my son would be fine and that sicklers are smart. She said that one of the good things was that nobody would be able to look at him and tell that anything was wrong with him. She told me not to be afraid that my son would die and to ask the Lord to heal him. She said if I believed it would be done, it would happen. The woman prayed for my family and encouraged me. I felt a great sense of relief and went back to William's room.

Over the next few days, William recovered and was sent home from the hospital. I felt guilty because I never asked the woman's name, and the hospital could not tell me who she was. I still think about that incident and will cherish the kindness she showed me for the rest of my life. I consider it a blessing from the Lord. This woman, through her actions, taught me the value of being kind to others. Paul says that we are to teach younger women to be kind, which means that we need to have a great deal of practice and experience with this attribute ourselves.

TO HAVE SELF-CONTROL

Paul identifies self-control as an attribute that older women need to teach younger women, because it takes time to develop. Every wife and mother needs to master this area of her life, and for me it was very difficult. I never viewed myself as a person who lacked self-control until I had my first orientation session on sickle-cell anemia. William was a little over a year old. Children's Hospital called and said it was time for me to go through an orientation session so that I would know how to care for my son. Bill didn't go because he had to work, and I felt I could tell him everything I learned when he got home.

I went to the orientation alone, and it devastated me beyond words. They showed me movies of children who were so sick they never left the hospital. They took me into the sickle-cell clinic and showed me children whose bones were deformed and turned backwards and others who were blind from sickling in their eyes. They took me to visit children in the hospital ward who had had strokes and were paralyzed from the neck down. In addition, they told me that this could happen to William. I was told that his disease did not have a cure, that William would live a shortened life, and that it would be decades before anyone would be able to do anything about sickle-cell anemia.

I loathed the day I had gone to that session. It haunted me in my dreams. My self-control begin to wane. I was panic stricken and nervous, and I became hysterical every time he needed to go to the hospital, which was often. I was angry at God for allowing me, a "good Christian" woman, to have a son (my only son) who had an incurable, excruciatingly painful disease. I lost all self-control, and not only that, I felt I was justified in doing so.

I wailed, yelled, and complained to God for over a year. Finally, three women of God decided that I needed discipling. They prayed for me, took me to conferences and retreats, had Bible studies with me, and stayed at the hospital with me when William was ill. They started a telephone prayer chain of people who prayed for my family regularly, especially when William was in crisis.

Although I was saved, they helped me to realize that I needed to repent for my attitude and lack of trust in God. I began to realize that my faith needed strengthening and I had to allow the Lord to take control of my life. That was the beginning of my rededication to the Lord and my new life under His control. The Lord transformed my life so dramatically that the panic attacks faded, I was not nervous, and my hysterical episodes stopped. Little did I know how much I would need self-control in the fourteen years that lay ahead. We faced countless trips to the emergency room, eleven life-threatening pneumonias, surgery, and eighty-three hospitalizations. I am able to share this victory because women who loved God took the time to disciple and prepare me for these years.

TO BE PURE

When I was a little girl, my favorite Bible verse was, "Blessed are the pure in heart, for they will see God" (Matthew 5:8), and I said it countless times before eating a meal. As I went through my last episode with William and sickle-cell anemia, I began to understand what the Scriptures meant by a pure heart. I also began to realize what it meant to grow through suffering and trials.

When William was fifteen years old and very ill, we discovered a boy who had received a bone marrow transplant and had been cured of sickle-cell anemia. We asked William's doctor about a transplant for him, and the doctor explained that his chances of finding a donor were very remote. He said that in order to get a bone marrow transplant as a sickler, you must have a perfect blood match from an identical twin or same-sex sibling. He knew that William was not a twin; in fact, William did not have a brother. The doctors said they had done thousands of tests across the country, and most people could not have this new treatment because finding a donor was nearly impossible. William's doctor told the story of a mother who had ten children, and none of them could provide a blood match for her child who had sickle cell.

I asked the church to pray, and everyone in our immediate family was tested as a potential donor. We had to wait two weeks for the results, and none of us could concentrate. Daily we prayed together, and we all tried to guess whom the Lord would choose as a match for William. We refused to let doubt creep into our minds. Finally, after two weeks of waiting, the nurse told us that our daughter, Crystal, who is two years older than William, was a perfect match for him, "just like an identical twin." Our family screamed, laughed, cried, and jumped for joy when we heard the news. We also marveled at the fact that the Lord had prepared a bone marrow donor for William two years before he was born. We celebrated, but the battle was just getting started.

The doctors told us we had to be sure about the transplant, because William was either going to be cured or die in the process—those were the choices. We did not have doubts about William's salvation. He had loved the Lord since he was a young child. William and our family made a decision to trust the Lord and go through with the transplant. We were told that William would be very sick. We were to expect vomiting, mouth sores, weight loss, hair loss, and loneliness from isolation. My challenge was to watch my son stand in the face of death as he went through the transplant. I went before the Lord in prayer and acknowledged with a pure heart that I trusted Him with my son, in life and in death. I also believed with a pure heart that God would cure my son.

One hundred days after the bone marrow transplant, William was declared cured of sickle-cell anemia by Children's Memorial Hospital in Chicago. At that time, only twenty-six people in the United States had been cured through a bone marrow transplant. Currently, he is a senior in high school, is on the track team, and is planning to attend college in the fall. We all suffered and went through trials that are too numerous to share, but now, for the first time, I can disciple wives and mothers who are facing painful illnesses and the possibility of death. I have been there, I understand, and the Lord is still teaching me new lessons. "Blessed are the pure in heart, for they will see God."

HOPE AND THE FUTURE

Today the reports that we read about the African-American home are overwhelmingly discouraging. The perception by some is that we do not have hope and a future. Yet the home is very significant to God, and He has made the wife and mother a key player in the primary socialization unit, the family. The importance of these roles creates a tremendous need for evangelism and discipleship. When African-American wives and mothers come to know Christ as their personal Savior and begin to live Christian lives, power is unleashed in families. This power is so great that it is capable of transforming the home, the community, our nation, and the world. It is within this context that we have hope for the future.

References

Hilliard, A. 1992. *The hidden light*. Houston: Hilliard.

June, S. 1996. *Women of color in the Bible and church history*. In *Women to women: Perspectives of fifteen African-American Christian women*, edited by N. Carter and M. Parker. Grand Rapids: Zondervan.

McKissic, W., Sr., and T. Evans. 1994. *Beyond* Roots II: *If anyone asks you who I am*. Wenonah, N.J.: Renaissance Productions.

Rainey, D., and R. Lewis. 1993. *Managing pressure in your marriage.* Ventura, Calif.: Gospel Light.

Santrock, J. 1996. *Child growth and development.* Madison: Brown & Benchmark.

Staley, S. 1996. *Bridging the gap: Mentoring younger women.* In *Women to women: Perspectives of fifteen African-American Christian women,* edited by N. Carter and M. Parker. Grand Rapids: Zondervan.

Williams, A. 1994. *Black man come home.* Memphis: Williams.

Wineberg, H. 1990. The timing of intermarital fertility. *Social Science Quarterly* 71 (March): 175–82.

CHRISTOPHER C. MATHIS JR.

Evangelizing and Discipling Youth and College Students

CHRISTOPHER C. MATHIS JR. is a doctoral candidate in agricultural and extension education at Michigan State University. He is a recipient of a Minority Competitive Doctoral Fellowship and serves as a graduate assistant in his department and in the office of the vice president of Student Affairs. He has been a resident hall coordinator for four years and a resident hall graduate advisor for three years. Born and reared in Newberry, South Carolina, Christopher holds a bachelor of science degree in biology and chemistry from Johnson C. Smith University and a master of arts degree in student affairs and higher administration from Michigan State University. He has a license of ministry from New Mount Calvary Baptist Church and ordination from the Word of Faith Bible Institute in Niamey, Niger, West Africa. He spent a year abroad as an international intern with Africare, under the International Foundation of Education Self-Help (IFESH) program, founded by Rev. Leon Sullivan. In addition, he is an associate minister and member of New Mount Calvary Baptist Church (Lansing, Michigan).

CHAPTER 10

CHRISTOPHER C. MATHIS JR.

Evangelizing and Discipling Youth and College Students

Train a child in the way he should go, and when he is old he will not turn from it. (Proverbs 22:6)

The rod of correction imparts wisdom, but a child left to himself disgraces his mother. (Proverbs 29:15)

When I was a child, I talked like a child, I thought like a child, I reasoned like a child. When I became a man, I put childish ways behind me. (1 Corinthians 13:11)

Remember your Creator in the days of your youth, before the days of trouble come and the years approach when you will say, "I find no pleasure in them." (Ecclesiastes 12:1)

INTRODUCTION

This chapter is written to stir the consciousness of African-Americans as to the importance of evangelizing and discipling youth in Christian principles and to offer ways in which this may be done. This topic is of critical importance, because how one is trained often determines one's contributions to society and community. This chapter will cover:

- The case and need for earlier training
- The challenges of discipling youth
- Youth ministries and their impact
- The importance of sound biblical training prior to college

139

- College ministries and their impact
- Resources and practical information

THE CASE FOR EARLIER TRAINING

Evangelism and discipleship involve training in a particular manner, custom, or tradition in order to ensure that a concept is continued. A *disciple,* according to Webster, is "a pupil or follower of any teacher or school of religion, learning, art, etc." The Greek word for disciple is *mathetes,* which means "a learner, to learn from a root, one who follows one teaching." Vine says a disciple is "not only a pupil, but an adherent; hence they are spoken of as imitators of their teacher" (1981, p. 316). A synonym for disciple is apprentice, a word defined by Webster as "a person under legal agreement to work a specified length of time for a master craftsman in a craft or trade in return for instruction."

Given these definitions, apprenticeship may be viewed as a forum for obtaining adequate training, exposure, and/or knowledge in a specific field of endeavor. Knowledge can be described as a medium of exchange of information, while training is a practice of imparting skills. Thus, one can think of a disciple as someone who is undergoing training for a specific length of time for a certain purpose.

Success does not happen by chance. It is increased when opportunity is given to an individual to be an apprentice to someone who has mastered a particular subject or craft. For example, the way Jesus transferred His skills and knowledge to His disciples was to draw them near to Himself, not only to hear Him teach, but to witness the teaching of His skills. This is probably why the disciples declared, "We cannot help speaking about what we have seen and heard" (Acts 4:20; see Bruce 1971), thus demonstrating that a disciple must have hands-on learning as well as verbal teaching. Consider this: If Jesus Christ had to train His disciples, what more should we be doing to ensure success among our youth and college students?

Frederick Douglass, in a speech during the West Indies Emancipation (August 4, 1857), declared the price of obtaining something (in this case freedom):

Those who profess to favor freedom, and yet deprecate agitation, are men who want crops without plowing up the ground. They want rain without thunder and lightning. They want the ocean without the

awful roar of its waters. This struggle may be both moral and physical; but it must be a struggle. Power concedes nothing without a
demand. It never did, and it never will.

Hence, the African-American community must be willing to risk personal
gain to sincerely train our youth and college students for a brighter
tomorrow.

THE CHALLENGES OF DISCIPLING YOUTH

Discipling youth is a challenge that can be intimidating. Many of us
have abandoned our responsibility of discipling youth and have given the
following reasons for doing so: "There is too much risk involved." "The
youth will not listen." "I'm too busy." "It's not my problem."

How many times have you heard these and similar phrases spoken
by someone in your community? Probably too often! Our once-support-
ive African-American community has weakened and is in danger of disappearing. Not only is community cohesion disappearing, but so are the
youth—at an alarming rate to drugs, gang-related deaths, Black-on-Black
homicide, and the penal system.

Curry (1991, p. 116) writes:

> In the past, Blacks benefited from more extended-family and neigh-
> borhood networks than today, that served to guide and nurture chil-
> dren. . . . But, as family members became more mobile and scattered
> geographically, and as predominately Black neighborhoods deterio-
> rated to the point where children live among "undesirable ele-
> ments," many of those supportive networks are no longer available.

Curry goes on to point out that "many of our children never get a chance
to be innocent, for they face harsh realities at a tender age" (p. 116). These
issues are more than reason enough for the Black community to seek
more accountability regarding the discipleship of its youth.

Proverbs 19:18 tells us that we should correct our youth while there
still is hope and that we should not be concerned whether they enjoy it,
for it is the right thing to do in God's sight. Allen (1996, pp. 35–36)
echoes this sentiment: "Choosing to risk time or effort to do what seems
difficult or impossible is never easy, yet without risk, many of the ameni-
ties that we take for granted today would not be possible: computers, television, radio, aircraft, electric lights, nuclear energy and automobiles."

Jesus says in Luke 9:24, "Whoever wants to save his life will lose it, but whoever loses his life for me will save it." This illustrates that we must be willing to take a risk and get involved with great seriousness, for without it one can easily predict the results.

If we ask God for His divine direction and seek His response, we will find a solution to effectively communicating with our youth. Most times it only takes a sincere effort on the part of the parent, mentor, etc., for the youth to listen and adhere to instruction and correction.

As a personal example, while serving as a resident hall director at a university, I volunteered to mentor "problem-gifted" youths at an alternative high school. I was assigned a Black male whom everyone feared. By taking an interest in this boy's well-being and through the grace of God and His divine Word, I was able to assist him in reentering the regular high school within fifteen months. It is time to stop making excuses for shrugging off our responsibilities. If we forfeit our commission to disciple youth, then who is to be blamed for their lack of commitment to family, community, and society as a whole? We are.

Proverbs 22:6 instructs: "Train a child in the way he should go, and when he is old he will not turn from it." The word *train* in Hebrew indicates being dedicated or devoted to something; or it may imply being prepared for the responsibilities one will have to take on as an adult. The phrase "in the way he should go" literally means "according to the way he acts," indicating that instruction is given to direct one in behavior. Thus, the quality of training a child receives is crucial to later development, underscoring the importance of proper training. Such a process can be referred to as the rites of passage.

The practice of rites of passages is thousands of years old and can be traced back to the continent of Africa, where boys ages fourteen to fifteen were taken from their tribal villages to "bush camps" for a period of four to five rains (rainy seasons or years). There they learned life skills and how to prove themselves worthy of manhood and marriage (Crowder 1983). Today such a formal training is not feasible in the original African tradition; however, the Black community must modify this training method to assist in the discipleship of youth. For example, Kunjufu (1989, p. 59) suggests that "we design programs that include an understanding of African history, spirituality, economics, politics, career development, citizenship, community involvement, and physical development that should operate within an African frame of reference and belief in *Nguzo-Saba,* a Black value system."

This point is further illustrated in Proverbs 29:15, which teaches that to avoid shame and reproach we must be willing to use the rod and reproof to give our youth wisdom to sustain them throughout life. If such a measure is not undertaken, we as a people shall reap what we have sown. Scripture tells us this in Galatians 6:7–8, underlining the significance of training (educating) our youth in the dictates of God's laws.

THE IMPACT OF YOUTH MINISTRIES

The Black church has always had a vital role in the educational advancement of its youth and is still paramount to ensuring their survival. The church is challenged with the responsibility of making its programs and ministries culturally and contemporarily relevant to real-life needs and issues. We must ensure that what we attempt to do has been sanctioned by God's Word or else it is in vain ("Unless the LORD builds the house, its builders labor in vain. Unless the LORD watches over the city, the watchmen stand guard in vain," Psalm 127:1).

Mbiti (1970, p. 3) shows how religion was an integral part of the whole of African life:

> Africans are notoriously religious, and each people has its own religious system with a set of beliefs and practices. Religion permeates into all the departments of life so fully that it is not easy or possible always to isolate it.

> African people do not know how to exist without religion. One of the sources of severe strain for Africans exposed to modern change is the increasing process (through education, urbanization and industrialization) by which individuals become detached from their traditional environment.

Mbiti points to the importance of incorporating God's Word into the daily aspects of our African-American life. To not do so means we are out of harmony with our African heritage. Therefore, parents and others who are entrusted to disciple (educate) our youth must make a conscious commitment to "disciple biblically."

One of the main problems in our communities is the tremendous lack of respect toward parents and elders. It was a past practice in South

Carolina—my home state—and in many other states to teach young people to respect their parents and elders. This was a major responsibility of the youth ministry, and when a young person failed to show respect, somebody would routinely correct him or her. Unfortunately, this type of training and accountability is viewed as obsolete. Could it be that we have allowed society too much latitude in influencing our decision about doing what "thus saith the Lord"?

We must teach young people how to respect their parents, for by doing so it gives them life. What I love about God's Word is that it repeats itself, indicating to us the importance of a particular concept. For example:

Deuteronomy 5:16 and Ephesians 6:1–3 state respectively:

> Honor your father and your mother, as the LORD your God has commanded you, so that you may live long and that it may go well with you in the land the LORD your God is giving you.

> Children, obey your parents in the Lord, for this is right. "Honor your father and mother"—which is the first commandment with a promise—"that it may go well with you and that you may enjoy long life on the earth."

These passages are confirming a principle as well as reiterating one of God's direct orders to young people. This is of significance to leaders of youth ministries, for when we fail to carry out God's commandants, there are severe negative consequences. Curry (1991, pp. 115–16) made this point:

> The proper educational development of children is an essential task for the church . . . which must join in with the family to counteract any inaccurate, self-defeating, or damaging messages their children may be receiving from the schools, their peers, or the media. The church must also seek ways to integrate the Christian faith and Christian learning with secular education. In order to develop spiritual leaders who are able to effectively teach, counsel, or guide others, the church must actively promote the study and mastery of academic disciplines.

Adults who are privileged to work with and around youth have a grave responsibility that should not be taken lightly, for we are entrusted to assist parents in the task of raising their child in a godly manner. The African proverb "It takes a village to raise a child" captures this challenge.

Youth ministries must also be properly staffed with personnel who are trained and qualified in order to ensure a well-designed, relevant, efficient, culturally and scripturally based curriculum. When this has not been the case, failure has been the result. It is vitally important that pastors endorse and financially support youth ministries if they are to have a significant impact.

SOUND BIBLICAL TRAINING PRIOR TO COLLEGE

Earlier I presented several Bible verses that indicate the importance God places on the proper training of children. Christians must, to the best of their ability, ensure that their children receive sound biblical training throughout early development. June (1991, p. 100) speaks to this issue: "To many, the ultimate responsibility for training children belongs unquestionably to parents. However, the erosion of family structures and transfer of control from the home to outside agencies warrant our taking another look."

It is of grave importance that Black parents regain control of discipling their offspring. We have witnessed for the past two decades the effects of not providing sound and systematic biblical training to our people. Scripture emphasizes over and over the mandate for sound and systematic biblical training and development. For example, Psalm 78:1–7 says:

O my people, hear my teaching;
  listen to the words of my mouth.
I will open my mouth in parables,
  I will utter hidden things, things from of old—
what we have heard and known,
  what our fathers have told us.
We will not hide them from their children;
  we will tell the next generation
the praiseworthy deeds of the LORD,
  his power, and the wonders he has done.
He decreed statutes for Jacob
  and established the law in Israel,
which he commanded our forefathers
  to teach their children,

so the next generation would know them,
> even the children yet to be born,
> and they in turn would tell their children.
Then they would put their trust in God
> and would not forget his deeds
> but would keep his commands.

Adults who know God's Word are expected to abide by it. We must seek to teach and train those born to us, as well as those we influence, sound biblical principles before they depart from their nurturing environment. As budding young adults go off to college, they will face challenges they have not dealt with prior to leaving home. Thus, if they have not had sound biblical training prior to this departure, the new environment may produce a devastating life experience.

Consider the following example given by Hillard (1995, p. 72).

> [A sheep dog] at birth is separated almost at once from. . .its family. . . .Then placed into a pen where there are nothing but sheep, including the young lambs who are nursing. In its normal drive to satisfy its hunger, it seeks out a ewe and tries to nurse from her, along with other lambs. When it is successful, it continues, and is then raised with sheep as a lamb until it is sufficiently developed to be trained. Notice here that it continues to look like a dog as well. . . .leave the track of a dog and have the speed and strength of a dog. Yet, while it has the intelligence of a dog, it will develop the mind of a sheep! Once that happens, it no longer acts like, or in the interest of itself as a dog, or in the interest of others dogs. . . .Moreover, it will see its own brothers and sisters as the "enemy" since this dog does not know them as brothers and sisters.

This story vividly depicts what occurs when someone is not trained properly by his or her group or family but rather is trained and nurtured outside of the family in an alien environment. Such training takes the person from a collective history and does not allow the "discernment" of the past nor the future. It leads to a development of dependency on others for knowledge, the inability to learn from the experience of one's group (race, religion, etc.), and the inability to communicate with one's group. These symptoms can be attributed to growing up in an alien environment that allows one to live in a world of illusions, seeing oneself as something that he or she is not. As Africans in North America, we have to awaken to the significance of affording our youth and college students sound biblical training prior to their departure into a new environment, for without it we await our final burial as a people.

THE IMPACT OF COLLEGE MINISTRIES

The first student Christian society dates back to 1706 at Harvard University (Shockley and Thurber 1995). By the end of the twentieth century, a considerable number of clergy were placed in colleges and universities to evangelize and disciple students, as well as to assist them with day-to-day life challenges. As times changed, however, so did the student ethnic makeup, their concerns, and the life challenges they had to attend to while obtaining a college education. Thus, college ministries must also diversify in order to meet the changing needs.

While college ministries such as Campus Crusade for Christ and Navigators seek to reach African-Americans, and do so with some effectiveness, much more needs to be done. Approximately 80 percent of African-American students are now on historically White campuses and are not being systematically evangelized or discipled. More culturally specific campus ministries must be developed, and African-American churches must partner with existing college ministries to aid in the spiritual, educational, physical, mental, social, cultural, and moral growth of African-American college students. College students are ill-equipped to handle real-life situations because they have been sheltered from reality and the knowledge of God's Word. Such improper training is not profitable to anyone: the student, the family, the church, the community, or society.

Mbiti (1970, pp. 3–4) indicates what college ministries (and all ministries) should be about:

> It is not enough to learn and embrace a faith which is active once a week, either on Sunday or Friday, while the rest of the week is virtually empty. It is not enough to embrace a faith which is confined to a church building or mosque, which is locked up six days and opened only once or twice a week.

> Unless Christianity fully occupies the whole person as much as, if not more than, traditional religions do, most converts to these faiths

will continue to revert to their old beliefs and practices for perhaps six days a week.

Mbiti's comments show the importance of having productive college ministries that will have a significant and lasting impact on their participants.

Curry (1991, p. 116) makes this point clear:

> The Black church is called upon to continue the plight of producing political, economic, social, and educational leaders. While formal education is not itself a sufficient element of Christian faith and belief, having educational tools better equips Christians to remain viable in a society that is ever increasingly complex and competitive. Reading, writing, mathematics, history, and other disciplines are essentials not only for occupational success, but also for understanding and teaching the Bible, its principles, and Christian service.

College ministries are faced with many of the same challenges as the Black church, for history and research have shown us that training impacts one's mental, physical, social, spiritual, and moral development. Just as Jesus trained His twelve disciples in all areas of life, so must we who are entrusted with the precious treasures of tomorrow's future. It is imperative that we "disciple biblically" our youth and college students, for failing to do so will lead to devastating consequences. Ayi Kwei Armah (1979, p. 71) echoes this sentiment: "A people losing sight of origins are dead, a people deaf to purposes are lost. Under fertile rain, in scorching sunshine there is no difference: their bodies are mere corpses, awaiting final burial."

RESOURCES AND PRACTICAL INFORMATION

There needs to be clear performance indicators to measure our effectiveness in "discipling biblically" our youth and college students for society's challenges.

To maximize evangelism and discipleship among youth and college students, I offer a brief listing of resources to assist in achieving this mission:

Bloy, Myron B., Jr. *Christian Identity on Campus* (New York: Seabury, 1971). Looks at the tradition of Christian identity in relation to pluralism and secularity on campus.

_____. *Community on Campus* (New York: Seabury, 1971). Explores the role of campus ministries in quest of community on campus.

Hare, Nathan, and Julia Hare. *Bringing the Black Boy to Manhood: The Passage* (1985). Available from African-American Images, 9204 Commercial Suite 308, Chicago, IL 60617. Contains procedures for conducting a rites-of-passage ceremony.

Hill, Paul, Jr. *Coming of Age: African- American Males Rites-of-Passage* (1992). Available from Black Think Tank, 1801 Bush Street, Suite 127, San Francisco, CA 94109. Contains a rites-of-passage training model.

June, Lee N., editor. *The Black Family: Past, Present and Future* (Grand Rapids: Zondervan, 1991). See especially Bonita Curry, "The Role of the Church in the Educational Development of the Black Child"; Shirley June, "The Role of the Home in the Spiritual Development of Black Children"; and Willie Richardson, "Evangelizing Black Males: Critical Issues and How-Tos."

Kunjufu, Jawanza. *Adam! Where Are You?* (1994). Available from African-American Images, 9204 Commercial Suite 308, Chicago, IL 60617. Describes why most Black men do not go to church.

_____. *Countering the Conspiracy to Destroy Black Boys,* vols. 1–5 (1985–95). Available from African-American Images, 9204 Commercial Suite 308, Chicago, IL 60617. Describes ways Black boys are targeted in the educational system, as well as ways to combat these efforts.

McCormick, Thomas R. *Campus Ministry in the Coming Age* (St. Louis, Mo.: CBP Press, 1987). Critiques campus ministries by examining their roots, vision, weakness, and success.

Richardson, Willie. *Reclaiming the Urban Family* (Grand Rapids: Zondervan, 1996). Shows how various programs of the church can assist families and also lists African-Americans who are resources on family issues.

CONCLUSION

The aims of this chapter have been:

- To stir the consciousness of African-Americans as to the importance of discipling and evangelizing youths and college students

- To challenge adults to "disciple biblically"
- To suggest that we put performance indicators into place
- To evaluate our efforts
- To offer resources to aid in discipling and evangelizing

The challenges of "discipling biblically" our youth and college students are apparent. Therefore, we must be willingly to provide financial support, sacrifice time, and risk personal gain to help youth develop into God-centered masterpieces who can effectively and willingly take on life challenges so as to ensure a godly presence in the twenty-first century.

It is my fervent and continual prayer that all who are entrusted to educate youth and college students commit themselves to "disciple biblically." The Holy Bible commands it, and the trying times demand it.

REFERENCES

Allen, H. L. 1996. Risk and failures as preludes to achievement. In *Men to men: Perspectives of sixteen African-American Christian men,* edited by L. N. June and M. Parker. Grand Rapids: Zondervan.

Armah, Ayi K. 1979. *Two thousand seasons.* Chicago: Third World Press.

Bruce, F. H. 1971. *The training of the Twelve.* Grand Rapids: Kregel.

Crowder, M. 1983. *Education for development.* Proceedings of a symposium held by the Botswana Society at the National Museum Art Gallery. Gabarone: Macmillan Botswana Publishing.

Curry, B. P. 1991. The role of the church in the educational development of Black children. In *The Black family: Past, present and future,* edited by L. N. June and M. Parker. Grand Rapids: Zondervan.

Hillard, A. G. 1995. *The maroon within us: Selected essays on African-American community socialization.* Baltimore: Black Classic Press.

June, L. N., and M. Parker, eds. 1996. *Men to men: Perspectives of sixteen African-American Christian men.* Grand Rapids: Zondervan.

June, S. 1991. The role of the home in the spiritual development of the Black child. In *The Black family: Past, present and future,* edited by L. N. June and M. Parker. Grand Rapids: Zondervan.

Kunjufu, J. 1994. *Adam! Where are you?* Chicago: Afro-American Publishing Co.

_____. Vol. 1, 1983; Vol. 2, 1985; Vol. 3, 1987; Vol. 6, 1995. *Countering the conspiracy to destroy Black boys*. Chicago: Afro-American Publishing Co.

Mbiti, J. S. 1970. *African religions and philosophy*. Garden City, N.Y.: Doubleday.

Richardson, W. 1996. *Reclaiming the urban family: How to mobilize the church as a family training center*. Grand Rapids: Zondervan.

_____. 1991. Evangelizing Black males: Critical issues and how-tos. In *The Black family: Past, present and future*, edited by L. N. June and M. Parker. Grand Rapids: Zondervan.

Shockley, D. G., and L. N. Thurber. 1995. Selected events in U.S. campus ministry history. *Journal of Ecumenical Studies* 32, no. 4.

Vine, W. E. 1981. *Vine's expository dictionary of Old and New Testament words*, edited by F. F. Bruce. Old Tappan, N.J.: Revell.

Webster's new ninth collegiate dictionary. 1985. Springfield, Mass.: Merriam-Webster.

PART FIVE

Going into the Field

JOSEPH C. JETER SR.

Help Wanted: Missionaries for the Harvest

JOSEPH C. JETER SR. was born in Philadelphia and is founder and president of Have Christ Will Travel Ministries, a faith mission based in Philadelphia with works in the United States, India, Haiti, Nova Scotia, and Liberia. Jeter is the author of several tracts, manuals, and books, including *Montrose Waite: Black Missionary Superb and the Father of Black Faith Missions.* He graduated from Philadelphia College of the Bible's Institute Evening School. He is a member of Corinthian Baptist Church in Germantown, Pennsylvania. He is married to Catherine Jeter, and they are the parents of five children: Diane Jeter Bryant, Dr. Rhonda Felice Jeter, Joseph C. Jeter Jr., Priscilla Jeter Iles, and Paul Emanuel Jeter, Esquire.

CHAPTER 11

JOSEPH C. JETER SR.

Help Wanted: Missionaries for the Harvest

INTRODUCTION

There is a need within the African-American church for missionaries who will evangelize and disciple both at home and abroad. At this point in our church history, parachurch groups are working with and through African-American churches to do the job of evangelism and discipleship but are seeing only minor results because they are misunderstanding the concepts of what a missionary is, what evangelism and discipleship are, and the importance of funding evangelism and discipleship programs and supporting missionaries.

I will cover each of these issues below. Then I will discuss the need for missionaries and the role of missionaries, and will end with personal comments on persons who have helped me in my journey as a missionary. First, however, I will share some information regarding home missionaries and mission agencies associated with the African-American church.

MISSIONARIES AND MISSIONARY AGENCIES ASSOCIATED WITH THE AFRICAN-AMERICAN CHURCH

There are only a few full-time home missionaries and mission agencies that are of African-American origin. There are also only a few African-American full-time missionaries working in our communities to do evangelism and discipleship. I will list some of those of which I am aware and the activities in which they are engaged.

- Neighborhood Crusades (Rev. Melvin Floyed), Philadelphia: Outreach to middle schools and high schools.
- Triple C Bible Camp, Bible Institute and Ministry (Rev. and Mrs. Vernon Watford), Ahoskie, North Carolina: Children's work, daily vacation Bible school, Bible clubs, Bible camp, church edification, teaching missionaries at the Bible institute.

- Light of the World Ministries (Rev. and Mrs. Sollers Jenkins), Wilson, North Carolina: Bible clubs, street meetings, discipleship training, vacation Bible schools, Bible institute.
- Have Christ Will Travel Ministries (Rev. and Mrs. Joseph C. Jeter, founders), Philadelphia: Bible clubs; *Ambassador Hour* radio broadcast, short- and long-term missionary training; sending of teens, adults, and seniors to home and foreign mission fields of the world. Nova Scotia, Haiti, and southwest India are some of the foreign fields. Philadelphia, Pittsburgh, New Jersey, and as far west as California are some of the home fields.
- Annette Smith (independent missionary), Atlanta: Bible clubs, teen clubs, prayer ministry, evangelism and discipleship training. Her outreach is rural and urban Georgia.
- Mixed ministries that do work in the African-American churches— for example, BCM International (Bible Club Movement) with Black missionaries in the Philadelphia area (Michelle Downs, Beverly Nottage, and others).
- Whosoever Will Gospel Mission of Philadelphia: Drug and alcohol rehabilitation in the Germantown area of Philadelphia.
- Home Missionary Agencies in Detroit and Chicago with Rev. Russ Knight and the urban outreach of the Keystone Baptist Church Wholistic Ministries.
- The American Missionary Fellowship: Upper Darby and Villanova, Pennsylvania.
- Rev. Marc Oden of Philadelphia and Wilmington, Delaware. He has a young people's work that is linked to a network of churches in Philadelphia and Camden and Newark, New Jersey, called Youth Spectacular.

Below are some of the churches of which I am aware that are open to missionary activity and have effective home mission programs:

- Christian Stronghold Baptist Church, Philadelphia (Dr. Willie Richardson, pastor)
- Prosperity Baptist Church, Los Angeles (Rev. Ray Rodgers, pastor)
- Bethany Baptist Church, Pittsburgh (Dr. William Glaze, pastor)
- Bethel Gospel Tabernacle, Hollis Queens, New York (Bishops Roderick Caesar Sr. and Jr., pastors)

- Mt. Zion Baptist Church, Los Angeles (Dr. E. V. Hill, pastor)
- New Song Bible Fellowship, Lanham, Maryland (Rev. Bernard Fuller, pastor)
- Kodish Church of Emmanuel, Pittsburgh (Dr. Barber, pastor)

There are obviously more than I can name in this chapter, but even if I were able to name all of them, there is still just a handful of churches that are open to missionaries being involved in evangelism and discipleship.

Because of the Southern Baptist Convention's push into the African-American community to recruit churches into their general program, many pastors that associate with the Southern Baptist Convention are now being exposed to what a missionary is and the missionary's role in evangelism and discipleship.

WHAT IS A MISSIONARY?

A missionary is one who is called and sent by the Lord Jesus Christ to spread and teach the gospel (Acts 1:8). He or she is sent by the Godhead to make known Jesus Christ, His salvation, a new way of life, and how to have fellowship with the Father, Son, and Holy Ghost (Mark 16:15–16).

The concept of a missionary in many churches is often quite different than that which the Bible teaches in the book of Acts. For example, many churches require missionaries to meet to raise money, to have a program every fifth Sunday in the year, to give out food at Thanksgiving and Christmas, and so on.

In the Bible, however, the missionary has a spiritual function as well as a physical one, that is, to make Jesus Christ known (Matthew 5:14), to have compassion, and to be laborers in the harvest (9:35–38).

The concept of evangelism in too many African-American churches is one of revival meetings, to which people come to hear an evangelist, as opposed to outreach evangelism, door-to-door outreach, or feeding programs with the idea of presenting Christ. In such churches there is no tract distribution, counseling, health fairs, basketball leagues, concerts, banquets, recreation activities, bus trips, picnics, or clothing distribution. At Triple C Bible Camp Ministries in Ahoskie, North Carolina, for example, Rev. V. Watford had a food pantry for the needy, a basketball league, and the Teen Scene (a program for teenagers) as means of sharing the gospel with the lost.

In Philadelphia, Gieger Memorial Brethren Church has the Master's Table on Saturday mornings from October to May to feed the inner-city crowd and present Christ. Missionary Ruby Hester was saved through that program and now works in it. She has never been to Bible school but was evangelized by their outreach and discipled by their ministry and is now a full-time missionary for and from that church where Rev. Anthony DiBenedetto Jr., a White person, is pastor.

Many years ago I evangelized in the Wayland Temple Baptist Church's (Philadelphia) Sunday school. I started a baseball team there in the late 1950s. Some of the leadership in that church today has its roots in that early ministry.

Thus, the concept of evangelism must be that of reaching out with the Good News of God's grace—salvation by grace through faith plus nothing (John 1:11–12; Romans 10:9–10; Ephesians 2:8–9).

THE CONCEPT OF DISCIPLESHIP AND EVANGELISM IN THE AFRICAN-AMERICAN CHURCH

A disciple is one who follows closely, hence a learner. The hymn writer, J. W. Harris, has penned a song entitled "I Want to Be a Follower of Christ" that adequately describes discipleship:

I want to be a follower of Christ,
I want to live in the newness of life.
What do I have to say?
I want to be a follower of Christ!

Discipleship is not simply finishing the new members' class, baptismal class, or stewardship training. It is much more. It is learning the practical principles of the Bible for Christian living, learning to love and live in obedience to the Lord Jesus Christ, and growing to be like Him. Discipleship training is the most important aspect of life for the new Christian and may be the weakest ministry in our churches.

When I was converted forty-nine years ago, I was told to live for Christ the best I knew how. I did not know much, but I had strong Christian examples. The deacons, the mothers of the church, and the Sunday school superintendent and staff all were spiritual. During that time, teaching and discipleship were more by example than by written words and class work. Today, however, we can reinforce what we see by the strong presentation of God's Word. Clearly, evangelism and discipleship training are the two most important programs in the church.

FUNDING THE PROGRAM

The attitude that the church has toward evangelism and discipleship funding will reflect the quality of the disciples it produces. One of the great problems for evangelism and discipleship training departments of the African-American church is finances. There are only a few churches other than the following that I know of that spend a large amount of money on evangelism and discipleship:

- Corner Stone Baptist, Oakland, California (Dr. L. L. Cannon, pastor)
- Christian Stronghold Baptist Church, Philadelphia (Dr. Willie Richardson, pastor)
- Progressive Baptist Church, Berkeley, California (Dr. Earl Stuckley, pastor)
- Mt. Zion Baptist Church, Los Angeles (Dr. E. V. Hill, pastor)
- New Song Bible Fellowship, Lanham, Maryland (Rev. Bernard Fuller, pastor)
- Oak Cliff Bible Fellowship Church, Dallas (Dr. Tony Evans, pastor)

MISSIONARY SUPPORT

This concept of the support of the missionary who will work in evangelism and discipleship is a major determinant of how effective the missionary will be in the church's program. Unfortunately, most will get little support and will spend more time at another ministry or get a job to support themselves. Thus, they will have less time to pray, prepare, and present the program (the gospel of salvation and gospel of edification).

ARE MISSIONARIES REALLY NEEDED IN THE AFRICAN-AMERICAN CHURCH AND COMMUNITY?

To some the answer is no. But I say *yes!* I will offer some proof for my answer by describing some of what has been done by missionaries working in the African-American church and community.

White home missionaries conducting weekday Bible clubs and morning and afternoon Sunday school in the "ghetto" of St. Louis, Missouri, at Blessed Hope Bible Church have seen many young people saved and have channeled those young people into the church to be discipled. Debra Perkins was saved, churched, discipled, and sent to Cedine Bible Institute (Spring City, Tennessee), and from there she was sent to Nova Scotia as a short-term missionary for Have Christ Will Travel Ministries. By faith she ministered to all races in the field with great success. Debra had picked up her burden for missions in the Bible club, Sunday school, and church in which she was discipled.

Home missionaries worked with the old American Sunday School Union (Philadelphia) in 1960 with the idea of strengthening the African-American churches and community in Philadelphia. During 1966 to 1972 an interracial team in inner-city Philadelphia effectively conducted afternoon Sunday schools to evangelize and disciple all ages. The outgrowth of that program helped the local churches. A discipleship leadership program was developed called Pioneers for Christ. The goal was to train young African-Americans to be leaders in evangelism and discipleship. The program was eventually stopped, but there were some positive results. For example, Diane Jeter Bryant went to Carver Bible College and became a full-time missionary in Nova Scotia for three years and served one year as a home missionary on the Have Christ Will Travel staff in Philadelphia. Dr. Leonard Thompson went to Philadelphia College of the Bible and became a pastor but is now a leader with the American Baptist Convention. Both of these people were involved with Pioneers for Christ.

Of course there are many others who have become outstanding Christians from this missions venture. The missionaries of this mission were committed to the church, and the results were positive. When funding was withdrawn, the program closed down. But the home missionaries were effective in Bible camps, Sunday schools, and discipleship and leadership training that blessed the local church. Some of the missionaries from that group were Rev. John Kim (Korea), Rev. Earl Moye (White American), and Rev. Howard Cartwright (African-American). Bill Brooks, a White American, directed that joint venture with the African-American churches in Philadelphia from 1966 to 1972. I also helped this mission, and we conducted vacation Bible schools all over Philadelphia. The American Sunday School Union supplied all of the Bible literature used.

THE ROLE OF THE MISSIONARY IN THE AFRICAN-AMERICAN CHURCH AND COMMUNITY

To plan and develop the program of evangelism for the church, there needs to be activities outside the church (outreach) and inside the church (inreach). The church is in the community and must be light. Matthew 5:14 describes the Christian as the light of the world and a city set on a hill. The role of missionaries is to let the light of the church shine in the community. Therefore, they must

- Pray for the tasks at hand (Luke 18:1)
- Inquire about the work (Nehemiah 1:2–3)
- Survey the task at hand, what they have, what they do not have, and what they need (Nehemiah 2:12–15)
- Accept the burden for the task at hand (Nehemiah 1:3–4)
- Plan a strategy

The following areas must be addressed:

Education—teaching
Poverty—clothing, food bank, etc.
Housing—do what you can
Visitation—food, literature, etc.
Gospel—Bible classes, teen clubs, recreation, tent meetings, street meetings
Home care, child care, etc.

In carrying out these duties, one must look with the eyes of Jesus, feel with the heart of Jesus, and give with the grace of Jesus. There is a need for discipleship (training, Bible classes, and leadership training) and teacher training Bible classes. Individuals involved in these programs must be built up by daily devotions filled with prayer, total dependence on the Lord (Colossians 1:18–19), and good works in their daily lives (Ephesians 2:10).

PERSONS WHO HAVE HELPED ME

In July 1960, while on vacation, I was called to preach the gospel of the Lord Jesus Christ. Within eighteen months I was pastoring a small storefront church in North Philadelphia while taking evening classes at Philadelphia College of the Bible. There I was exposed to missionaries, and the fire began to burn. One day as I was cleaning the front of the church, Viola Reddish came down the street and spoke to me. "Are you the pastor?" she asked. I said yes. She told me that she was a missionary on leave from her field in Liberia, West Africa, and a teacher at the Lehigh Elementary School. She needed a place to hold a Bible club for the children in that school who wanted to know about Jesus Christ, and she asked if she could use our church on Thursday afternoons. I said yes. Every Thursday she walked these children eight blocks to the church and then back to the school.

This was the beginning of missionary discipling for us. She joined our church and for two years taught much about Africa. Then she returned to Liberia, West Africa, where she died in the Lord's service in 1970 at ELWA Hospital near Monrovia, Liberia, with her vision fulfilled to disciple my wife, Catherine, and me as missionaries.

The life of Viola Reddish influenced my wife and daughter Diane to go into missions and through them my other four children, Rhonda, Priscilla, Joseph, and Paul, who served as short-term missionaries as we pioneered in Nova Scotia in the late 1960s and 1970s.

The ministries of missionary evangelist Ernest Wilson and Rev. Montrose Waite of Philadelphia also had dramatic effects on me and on discipleship in the churches in Philadelphia, Cleveland, and other areas of this country.

Rev. Waite came to Philadelphia in the mid-1940s and stirred the hearts of pastors and worked with churches to disciple them for world missions. His vision was for African-American Christians to be used by the Lord Jesus Christ in world ministry (for a biography of his life, see Seals and McNeal 1988).

Rev. Wilson also made Philadelphia his headquarters during this time period and worked with churches in the area as well as internationally in places such as Kenya, Uganda, the Caribbean, and Central and South America.

At the time of these two men of God, only the Black denominations in America and a few independent Black missionaries (who did not qualify or meet the standards of the denominations but had the call of God on their lives) could and did minister in world missions. God had raised the independent faith missionaries to go, and they did. They were ordinary Christians who heard God's call and said, "Here am I. Send me!" (Isaiah 6:8).

Wilson and Waite were determined to work as missionaries with the churches to disciple them for world missions. They, Ben Johnson, and others began Afro-American Missionary Crusades in Philadelphia. Because of them, African-Americans like Martha Thompson and Dorothy Evans served twenty years or more in Liberia. A second mission board, Carver Foreign Missions of Atlanta, was begun by Rev. Waite and Rev. Talmago Paine, a White man. They sent Naomi Doles from Hampton, Virginia, and Cora McCleary, from Chattanooga, Tennessee, to work in Liberia.

Wilson and Waite also had a profound effect on my wife and me. At Wilson's invitation and the call of the Lord Jesus Christ, I went to East Africa (Uganda) in 1965. This mission to Uganda opened the world for me, and in 1966 I made my first trip to Liberia for ministry. During the time of these men's ministry, the White leadership in missions refused to use African-American Christians as missionaries. Through the ministries of Waite, Wilson, and Viola Reddish, however, Have Christ Will Travel Ministries was born. Our mission now works in West Africa, the West Indies, Nova Scotia, Kerala State in southwest India, and the United States. The discipleship of these faithful servants of God also brought about our mission's Short-Term Ministries Department, which has sent out young, middle-aged, and older African-American Christians around the world for thirty years. My wife, Catherine, is director of the Short-Term Ministries Department.

CONCLUSION

Missionaries in the African-American church must assist the church in evangelism and discipleship, must be empowered by the Holy Spirit with a vision for evangelism, must implement a program of discipleship, and must reap that harvest. Missionaries must remember what Jesus did in Matthew 9:36–38—that is, He looked with compassion, saw the people and the harvest, and instructed His disciples to pray for laborers (for a discussion of the importance of prayer, see Jeter 1995).

Churches in the African-American community must likewise assist the missionary in his or her attempts to spread the gospel. The financial and spiritual support of the churches would greatly enhance their effectiveness in building the kingdom of God.

REFERENCES

Jeter, J. C., Jr. 1995. Prayer in leadership. In *Call to lead,* edited by E. Seals and M. Parker. Chicago: Moody Press.

Seals, E., and J. McNeal Jr., editors. 1988. *Waite: A man who could not wait.* Atlanta: Carver Foreign Missions.

HENRY LEE (HANK) ALLEN

Evangelizing Professionals: Workers in the Field

HENRY LEE (HANK) ALLEN is associate professor of sociology at Wheaton College. He has a biblical studies degree from Wheaton College and a doctor of philosophy degree from the University of Chicago. Born in Joiner, Arkansas, and raised in Phoenix, Illinois, he is married to Juliet Cooper Allen. They have eight children: Jonathan, Jessica, Janice, Justin, Julia, Janel, Joseph, and Judith. Hank is actively involved at Bethel Full Gospel Church in Rochester, New York. He has served on the faculty at Bethel College (Minnesota) and Calvin College (Michigan), University of Rochester, and Rochester Institute of Technology.

CHAPTER 12

HENRY LEE (HANK) ALLEN

Evangelizing Professionals: Workers in the Field

INTRODUCTION

Our world is increasingly characterized by technological complexity, social diversity, and persistent inequalities within and between countries (Rifkin 1995). Market fluctuations reflect these ubiquitous phenomena (Frank and Cook 1995). Industries and organizations are undergoing restructuring and downsizing to confront these multiple realities. As societies undergo global transformations in the compositions of their occupational structures, those persons who perform professional duties become more crucial to the operation of nations. Economic and technological transformations favor the service sector jobs occupied by professionals. Advances in educational attainment are mediated by the expertise possessed by professionals. Whether in the public, private, or nonprofit sectors, professionals dominate the fields of medicine, science, government, economics, law, business, education, religion, and communications. Even the armed forces are characterized by professional agents, structures, and processes. In essence, the postindustrial world is organized around the activities of professionals (Abbott 1988).

Professionals pursue their business by producing a body of expertise or practice that is useful to the society in which they are located. Professionals therefore have a very strategic role in evangelizing and discipling the nations of the world. First, they can be the objects of evangelistic efforts as they hear and respond to the gospel of Christ. Second, as disciples, they can be conduits of the gospel message when they interact with family, friends, other professional colleagues, and others as they travel throughout the occupational and geographical spheres of the world. Third, professionals can aid in world evangelization by producing valuable expertise and resources that are instrumental to discipling people from all walks of life. Finally, professionals can create or manage ministries whose aim is the proclamation and inculcation of

Christ's gospel. In all these ways, professionals can play a decisive role in world evangelization.

The focus of this chapter is African-American professionals who are located in or originate from the United States. Collectively, these African-American professionals represent a profound repository of the best ideas known; they could also be a magnificent pool of resources and knowledge that could affect the world through evangelism and discipleship. Many African-American professionals are actively serving as community leaders, civic authorities, church officials, volunteers, and philanthropists in addition to functioning as responsible role models for families and youth to emulate. African-American agencies or communities would crumble precipitously without the sustained involvement of professionals. In no way then can African-American professionals be neglected as the objects or conduits of the gospel. Their influence is both pervasive and strategic as we engage the twenty-first century.

This chapter will explore the legacy of African-American professionals in order to visualize their pivotal role in accelerating Christ's rule and reign in the lives of women and men everywhere. First, I will describe important social features influencing the relational and cultural worlds in which all African-American professionals participate, items that affect their role identity, vision, and socialization. Next, I will highlight the enormous potential African-American professionals have as a prelude to establishing their awesome responsibilities with respect to evangelism and discipleship within and outside their domiciles. Last, I will delineate a few essential motifs or vital aspects critical to evangelizing and discipling professionals.

THE SOCIOLOGICAL WORLD OF AFRICAN-AMERICAN PROFESSIONALS

In recent decades African-American professionals have emerged in society, having battled the vestiges of racism, inequality, and segregation in order to assume their decisive role in their communities. According to census data, African-American professionals have increased from 5.6 percent of all managerial and professional workers employed in 1983 to 7.4 percent of all such workers in 1996 (Statistical Abstract of the United States 1997). Restricted to professionals alone, African-Americans have increased in employment from 6.4 percent in 1983 to 7.9 percent in 1996.

Consequently, of the 18,752,000 professionals employed in the United States during 1996, an estimated 1,481,408 were African-American.

The sociological world of African-American professionals may be analyzed by considering its relational and cultural aspects. On the relational side, all African-Americans have various familial, kinship, or social ties with persons within as well as outside their ethnic group. This network of lifelong human relationships may be close or distant, informal or formal, public or private, or long-term versus short-term in nature. These relations can occur in friendships, peer groups, communities, voluntary associations, or bureaucracies. African-American professionals are shaped (for better or worse) by their own decision-making processes, communication patterns, and exposure within the context of their social ties. This set of social ties represents the social capital that helps them cope as a "minority" population in this multiethnic society. African-American professionals therefore possess a relational heritage.

Every ethnic group also has a valuable cultural heritage that encodes and decodes the information, behavior, tastes, expectations, values, beliefs, and perceptions bequeathed to its members. Hence, African-American professionals—whatever their occupational category—participate within an ongoing cultural legacy, passed from generation to generation, from place to place. One can readily observe this legacy in music and food, in hair care and entertainment, in styles of dress and artistic expressions, in preferences and interests. No professional can escape the symbolic capital he or she inherits from his or her cultural origins. While other ethnic groups might invariably use it to evaluate our merits or assess our worth, our cultural background often provides the opportunity for creative expression and innovation in the endeavors of life. Thus, African-American professionals collectively shoulder serious responsibility for either enhancing or detracting from the cultural capital they have received.

All professionals exist in an occupational milieu that is characterized by its own unique set of symbols, communication patterns, and role demands. There are a variety of formal and informal patterns of social interaction in every single professional domain—as can be readily seen among doctors, lawyers, engineers, and professors. Consequently, the cultural world of African-American professionals encompasses a number of visible and invisible dimensions. Contemporary magazines (such as

Ebony, Jet, Emerge, and *Essence*) and media extol the overt prestige and affluence of African-American professional life before the populace. Indeed, any legitimate attainment of professional status should be applauded in a society where the social networks and opportunity structures favor historically advantaged ethnic groups. African-Americans of every social status can therefore take delight in the collective achievements of their experts and celebrities, for these achievers have triumphed against enormous odds: their pains and fame have brought us multiple, yet enduring, gains.

At the visible level, therefore, African-American professionals have achieved this society's most treasured occupational statuses or careers. They hold key positions of influence and power in business and government. They serve as educated role models for younger generations of African-Americans. They are the key nodes in a network of social contacts that facilitate social mobility within and outside their communities. As the best and the brightest African-Americans, these professionals are the guardians of future expertise, thereby embodying the hopes and aspirations of many generations of African-American professionals from all walks of life. For many other ethnic communities as well, African-American professionals function as vital stewards in this society.

However, at the invisible level, African-American professionals and their families often pay severe costs to acquire this exalted status. The cultural world inhabited by African-American professionals can be very competitive and stressful at times, even if it provides many material as well as intangible rewards. Multitudinous pressures abound from a variety of domains and constituencies simultaneously. Such complicated demands often impose limitations on the time and energy African-American professionals are able to invest in personal activities. Family and other significant relationships can suffer under these restraints too. Being busy and being professional are too frequently synonymous occurrences.

Social changes can complicate the hectic lives of diligent professionals. Obviously, population size and demographic trends affect the demand for professional expertise. Emergent cultural trends require cyclical or systematic adjustments. For instance, all African-American professionals are affected by popular ideological perceptions about merit. External pressures come from changing social structures and role responsibilities. Political fluctuations can decisively shape the opportunity structures African-American professionals encounter in government, business, and education. Internal pressures come from their normal developmental needs and duties. Marital and family responsibilities do not disappear as occupational endeavors escalate. Moreover, aging processes and financial needs are ubiquitous to all workers.

Several ecological reasons account for the endemic stress that accompanies the benefits of professionalism. First, these active professionals must compete successfully in a global marketplace where there is stiff, intense competition from similar professionals from other ethnic groups. Life in the corporate, legal, academic, or medical professions can be very arduous, as the hydra of multiple demands tug at the sanity and sensibilities of any busy person. The rapid pace of current technological changes threatens all professionals, often making the expertise they have acquired across many laborious years somewhat obsolete. The sheer number of competitors is also a factor within a professional career.

Second, there is the perennial pressure of productivity that affects the destiny of all professionals. Expertise increases at an exponential rate in shorter and shorter time periods, thereby putting pressure on professionals to stay current with the latest and best advancements in their chosen endeavors. Besides this, the reward for success among clients is most often more clients and other leadership opportunities. Given the limits of time, professionals can be simultaneously plagued by both the tyranny of the urgent and the urgency of planning to handle future demands. Even though professionals enjoy their work tremendously, there is an inherent limit to their human capacities—cognitive, emotional, social, or physical.

There are, third, spiritual limits to professional success. Many successful professionals eventually discover that higher incomes and career rewards cannot fulfill the deepest longings of the human heart. Worldly acclaim is ephemeral; status lasts only as long as a person can avoid catastrophic mistakes. Failure typically brings vehement ridicule, rejection, and isolation. Professional life is instrumental to one's identity, but it is not a viable substitute for vision (life purpose), a sense of belonging, self-worth, or loving relationships. Everyone on this planet—whatever her or his ethnic origins—needs sustenance and redemption. Professional status does not insulate its recipients from the individual or combined effects of worldliness, depravity, or weakness. Neither does it offer any salvation from decay and death. For all these and other reasons, African-American professionals need to be involved in evangelistic efforts designed to link their lives with the supernatural power and resources available in Christ.

THE TREMENDOUS POTENTIAL OF AFRICAN-AMERICAN PROFESSIONALS

Evangelism and discipleship are pivotal to mentoring African-American professionals, inoculating them from (1) the achievement syndrome; (2) the success syndrome; (3) the pride, popularity, or celebrity and pleasure syndromes; (4) the organizational syndrome; (5) the pressure syndrome; and (6) the character syndrome. Each of these syndromes can poison the happiness of African-American professionals and their families if left unabated. To these phenomena we briefly turn our attention to show the necessity of evangelism and discipleship for sustaining the best features of professional life. Unfortunately, in recent years many famous African-American professionals have become the victims of any number of syndromes listed above.

Achievement syndrome. The United States is infested with the achievement syndrome for men and women, rich and poor alike. If a human being's most precious indigenous possession is his or her self-image (a refection of being made in the image of Almighty God), then the achievement syndrome may be a more lethal threat than a heart attack. The achievement syndrome evaluates persons' worth based on what they have done or can accomplish; it is often the legalistic by-product of overindulging the notion of meritocracy. We become best acquainted with this syndrome when siblings of different abilities are compared in families, or when children with heterogeneous interests or capacities are compared by the same standards in schools. As one ascends the hierarchy of the educational system and then enters the professional world, he or she can insidiously inculcate the pernicious assumptions endemic to this syndrome. The Lord taught that the life of persons never consists in what they possess, a poignant truth that includes intangible possessions like achievements as well as material resources.

Christ demonstrated repeatedly to His critics that the worth of persons is not contained in what they do or fail to do; self-worth is bequeathed to all humans by God Himself. The achievement syndrome confounds self-worth and competence, implying that your worth is instrumental to your achievement rather than vice versa. The achievement syndrome appears when false, ridiculous expectations or standards of judgment prevail. It may conceal an incipient self-righteousness that only the gospel can fully assuage. Many professionals live under the burden of perfectionism, suffering an inordinate collapse when they fail, addicted to an internalized psychological taskmaster every bit as worse as slavery. The gospel certifies that your inherent worth as a human being in Christ's kingdom is independent of what you could ever accomplish professionally or otherwise because Christ has already accomplished your salvation by His sacrificial death, and He works greatly through His Holy Spirit to assist you supernaturally to fulfill all your good works.

The gospel relieves the pressure of professionalism; it liberates persons from having to prove their worth to others by the gauntlet of performance. Moreover, Christ provides the wisdom necessary to be productive via the Bible. One gains the best of professional life by losing it to Christ's jurisdiction. One gains His supernatural presence, help, resources, and power to fulfill one's duties. He will also restore our losses and heal our deepest wounds. In Christ, our achievements are treasured as yardsticks to spiritual maturity, not the building blocks of insecurity. Surely this is the greatest news any honest and open professional can ever have.

Success syndrome. The gospel of Christ helps professionals to see their privileges as opportunities to focus on service as the essence of their work, to view their expertise and influence as a divine stewardship or fiduciary responsibility. This ethical stance, the fallout of the gospel, militates against the success syndrome, a perversion of the gratitude we should have for all the blessings God allows us to enjoy. The success syndrome is evident as one replaces her or his opportunities for generosity and gratefulness with the never-ending quest for individual attainment. African-American professionals must avoid the mythology of the self-made person, the idolatry of materialism, and the ideology of celebrityhood. All success has a price tag. Often, loved ones are left to pay the price of a penchant for too much selfish gain. To enjoy righteous success, African-American professionals must not focus on acquiring more wealth, prestige, and power; rather, they must relate their professional ambitions to evangelism and discipleship. Using the spiritual gifts they have, their dominant concern must shift from merely impressing people to impressing God. Consequently, societal fetishes with beauty, popularity, self-gratification, and rebellion must be exterminated mentally and spiritually. Pride and deception must be vanquished by a crucified life. Wrong ideas about success can erode our vision, cause us to compromise our values, attenuate our virtue, and deceive us into losing our need for God and others. Again, Christ's gospel is the remedy for spiritual decay.

Pride, popularity, or celebrity and pleasure syndromes. Rather than become intoxicated by the seductions of the success syndrome, African-American professionals can seek to reproduce themselves in the lives of those who need or admire them. Such a task is effective therapy and could help guard against the pride syndrome, the condition that exists whenever any professional becomes a legend in his or her own mind. The pride syndrome may be likewise connected to the desire for fame (the popularity syndrome); it can result in an additional yearning for pleasure (the pleasure syndrome). The lives, marriages, and families of many professionals have been ruined by the coalescence of these maladies. As the gospel is shared by their colleagues via evangelism and discipleship, it can reveal to all African-American professionals the awesome power of humility, the preciousness of solitude, and the pleasantness of contentment, as well as peace. When one acquires these spiritual riches as an antidote for corresponding syndromes, no other craving can distract or satisfy.

Organizational syndrome. The organizational syndrome occurs whenever professionals unduly restrict their lives to the places where they are employed. It is frequently based on a reductionistic view of life and work. Professionals can easily become so engulfed in their work activities that they become totally oblivious to the needs of significant others located outside their companies. Many find out the hard way that superficial organizational ties are not sufficient to replace the full realm of relational and cultural ties a person acquires throughout life.

Pressure syndrome. The pressure syndrome convinces African-American professionals that they must work twice as hard as someone else to survive, an unbiblical injunction to rely on their own efforts rather than the sovereignty of Almighty God. The gospel of Christ releases a professional from the prison of someone else's expectations because no weapon formed against His children will prevail against the backdrop of eternity; sin has a built-in destructive consequence even in the hands of the worst oppressors. Unless they respond to the gospel, the worst oppressors will spend eternity reaping the same oppression that they have planted in our lives. Ask Pontius Pilate, Herod, or Judas Iscariot—if you could. The diabolical syndrome of racism itself cannot ultimately succeed against the kingdom of God as all will one day behold.

Character syndrome. Each of the syndromes identified above affect character, our internal predispositions to respond to life's situations. The character syndrome is linked to the pervasive reality that many successful African-American professionals have repeatedly fallen into public disgrace or disrepute at the pinnacle of their success. All too often their highly visible lives are indicted by horrendous scandals, corrupted by superfluous appetites, and enraptured by vain delusions. The catalog of names is much too burdensome to reiterate. Without the gospel, professionals are very susceptible to the most degrading circumstances imaginable as multitudes of people observe their sinful folly.

Whatever the syndrome, whatever the predicament, Christ can bring the best from the worst, the strongest from the weakest, the most from the least. That is why every professional needs to encounter the gospel as it is transmitted from person to person via evangelism and discipleship. There is no greater news in this pressured world, no greater hope for the future regardless of the complexity, inequality, diversity, and apostasy that encroaches anywhere.

In this section I have endeavored to explain why the gospel of Jesus Christ remains relevant to African-American professionals today. I do not want to convey the erroneous impression that the benefits of professional life fail to exceed its enormous costs. Professional life need not be all doom and gloom! The gospel of Jesus Christ gives the good news and supernatural power needed by all professionals to cope with the manifold joys and duties of their careers. God sent Christ to vitiate our obstacles, to confound our foes, to help us in our areas of weaknesses, to forgive our wrongs, to recover our losses, and to assuage our injustices. When manifested through effective evangelism and discipleship, the gospel of Christ can help African-American professionals to escape the various, sometimes inconspicuous, syndromes or pitfalls that could afflict them.

EVANGELIZING AND DISCIPLING AFRICAN-AMERICAN PROFESSIONALS

Having established a brief rationale for evangelism and discipleship among African-American professionals, the task before us now is to specify how to conduct each spiritual activity. Evangelism should be the natural outgrowth of a healthy relationship with Christ and the members of His church. Discipleship simply means to be a disciplined learner under the tutelage of a more experienced exemplar. Together they constitute a dynamic duo for those whose intent is to spread the gospel of salvation in Christ. Yet each has a unique contribution to make to the destinies of African-American professionals. Evangelism declares the good news about Christ's atoning sacrifice and confronts unbelievers with the enduring claims of the gospel. Discipleship brings the gospel to all areas of a convert's life.

It is axiomatic to orthodox believers everywhere that persistent intercessory prayer is a prerequisite to both evangelism and discipleship. Prayer places the evangelistic initiative where it belongs (with the Holy Spirit) and invites the professional—who serves as the conduit of the gospel—to submit to the ongoing enterprise of God. A wise professional prays incessantly for an opportunity to tell his or her colleagues about Christ. He or she acts in response to divine prompting instead of unwittingly shoving the gospel down another's throat. Christ never employed any underhanded extortions or cute manipulations in revealing His deity to sinners. Professionals who engage in evangelism must be careful to accentuate the positive aspects of unbelievers (John 3:17) even as they concurrently reveal the desperate plight of those who ignore or reject Christ (John 3:16).

To begin with evangelism—defined simply as telling others the good news of Christ's coming, atoning sacrifice, and resurrection—I would advise that one should model the supernatural love of the gospel as one tells others about Christ. Professionals need love whether or not they respond favorably to the claims of the gospel. True love manifests itself first in the joys of friendship. Hence, evangelism begins with friendship, a loving acceptance and concern for the welfare of a professional colleague. We must enter another person's world, understanding life from his or her point of view and empathizing with that person's struggles. This entails having integrity about one's life experiences and testimony even to the point of admitting what one does not know. Even when mistakes are made, sincerity permits recovery. Love does not engage in deception or manipulation. Our task is to tell others about Christ, informing them about how He has transformed our lives—not sell Him like a useless commodity. Friendship evangelism cannot be executed without allowing oneself to be vulnerable to hurt feelings, resistance, and misunderstanding.

Sociologists have long recognized that any person can be influenced by symbolic interactions with another person or group. A symbolic interaction occurs whenever two individuals directly or indirectly exchange speech, gestures, writings, behavior, and any other message between themselves. In short, we humans are always being affected by those with whom we interact on a recurrent basis. The more we interact with others, the more similar our joint interests or endeavors can become. Furthermore, successful interactions encourage a cycle of positive social exchanges in both mental and tangible goods. Friends often exchange ideas, resources, and social capital. Hence, friendship evangelism is the fulcrum of discipleship.

As good friends, we must be visible to and involved with unsaved professionals in our field—no matter how difficult this may be. Professionals can often hide behind the cloak of expertise or the artificial veneer of status when confronted by the authentic claims of the gospel, for the very reasons elaborated in the syndromes highlighted above. Our sacrificial love as friends must endure long enough to bring sustained conviction to the unsaved person behind the facade. Integrity gives the unconquerable radiance and authenticity needed to penetrate the mental roadblocks erected against the gospel. Based on this platform of a loving friendship, one can invite an unbelieving professional to meet other believers, whether at another professional meeting, church, or social gathering.

Believers must always be alert to unexpected invitations or opportunities to proclaim the gospel of Jesus Christ to their unsaved colleagues. They must also be aggressive or bold in asking them to commit their lives to the risen and exalted Christ; no apologies are needed. From sustained interaction with the Christ who indwells every believer, an unsaved professional should become increasingly aware of what is missing in her or his domain. This realization should prompt a desire either to learn more about Christ or, sadly, to become less amenable to the gospel. Delays or uncertainty could also be possible as a person carefully ponders a decision affecting his or her eternal fate. Here, at this point, the virtue of a godly example by the professional responsible for evangelization may assuage doubts.

Discipleship is the outcome of sustained socialization via collegiality, mentoring, or sponsoring ties. As Titus 2 envisions, older disciples are supposed to act as mentors for their younger counterparts. The former should assist in expanding the latter's fledgling biblical knowledge, spiritual maturity, and moral accountability. Mature disciples can likewise aid new believers in expanding their level of professional expertise as well as enhancing the range of social contacts. Discipleship encompasses mutual reconciliation and restoration, mediation, and prayer. Each follower of Christ is morally responsible for encouraging another disciple to reach his or her potential and fulfill his or her destiny in Christ. All too often, this vital ministry is seriously neglected among African-American professionals in Christ.

Discipleship must include regular encounters to be effective. Consequently, availability is crucial to its success. Discipling is a social process whereby the depth (rootedness) as well as breadth (scope) of nurturing ties must be inculcated as much as possible over time. Interactions might reasonably include prayer, biblical studies, confession, reconciliation, service, accountability, and other creative expressions of encouragement. Ultimately, these systematic meetings must involve formal and informal exchanges in a variety of social venues—among family, community, church, and elsewhere. The fundamental aim is to develop a relationship between mentor and pupil that is characterized by genuine reciprocity under the authority of Christ Himself. To wit, a submissive demeanor is imperative; cordiality, too, is essential. Companionship and competence must be stressed, along with the usual spiritual verities. Discipline of time and effort are therefore instrumental to discipleship and essential for godliness. Discipleship implies perpetual learning.

At times discipleship might involve crossing denominational barriers, especially in professional areas where believers are scarce or where organized discipleship networks are nonexistent. Evangelicals, Pentecostals, and other devoted Christians might be forced to find common ground in professional arenas where apostasy and secularism engulf all. Those who wish to be discipled should be flexible enough to seek out exemplars from a plethora of church backgrounds as long as these persons exemplify the character of Christ, confessing Him fully by orthodox words, motives, character, and deeds. Too often the magnification of unbiblical distinctions or traditions among believers can rob disciples of potential opportunities for spiritual togetherness.

I will end this section by giving personal reflections and specifying a vision for what could be done to further evangelism and discipleship among this generation of professionals. I have been involved in many different types of evangelistic efforts and discipleship relations in my thirty years as a follower of Christ. For me, evangelism is best accomplished when it is the overflow of joy in Christ, whether in good or distressful times. The best method of evangelism is often to testify—by word or deed—about why you have come to love and serve the Lord, especially when your life stimulates another person to ask you about why you have become a Christian. We believers ought to be excited everyday about our salvation in Christ. Just tell others what you know and have experienced in Christ.

One must conquer the multiple fears of failure, ridicule, doubt, or inadequacy by realizing that no personality, status, or intellect is required to be effective in evangelism—for it is the indwelling Holy Spirit's job to use your abilities to tell others about the good news of Christ's coming. Realizing that the Holy Spirit empowers you to evangelize effectively, whatever the situation, should take the onus off you and remove fear. Those who are ready to embrace Christ as Savior will be drawn to you under the guidance and timing of the Holy Spirit. The New Testament is replete with the different ways God has used quite different personalities or occupations in evangelizing others, especially in the book of Acts. Nonetheless, every disciple—where possible—should learn or adopt effective techniques for communicating his or her faith in Christ. The formal study of apologetics and books about evangelism should be consulted by all professionals in this information age.

Regarding discipleship, my experiences before marriage and career were much more effectual. Back then I was exposed to parachurch organizations that aggressively sought to extend the ministry of discipleship. Since graduate school, that level of contact has greatly diminished, ostensibly because the discipleship networks among African-American professionals tend to be sporadic, diffuse, localized, isolated, and disconnected.

Outside of local church ties, professionals in the very same organization or locality might not even know of the existence of each other. There needs to be a coordinated strategy to establish national, regional, and local discipleship networks for professionals of all ages as we enter the twenty-first century. I currently yearn for the deliberate organization of discipleship networks among African-Americans in every professional field of endeavor, especially the academic professions.

My heartfelt advice to all those doctors, lawyers, businesspersons, and other professionals who are committed to evangelism and discipleship is that we need to organize mentorship and sponsorship organizations (whether formal or informal) much more systematically than we have done thus far in order to give added efficiency to our individualized efforts. Organization is desperately needed within separate professions as well as between them. We can start these entities locally, strategize within them regionally, and unify them nationally in order to build momentum for the next generations. I even dare to dream of a Christian Academy of Sciences or Society of Christian Professionals to facilitate this vision someday soon. We must dream and act as big as our God in His infinite greatness will allow. Our disjointed efforts at evangelism and discipleship would receive much needed synergism from the collective organization of our professional endeavors.

CONCLUSION

African-American professionals today have a determinative role to perform in the spreading of the gospel similar to Joseph in Egypt, Daniel in Babylon, Esther in Persia, Lydia in Philippi, and Luke. God wants to use modern professionals to advance His kingdom on earth just like the afore-mentioned members of the hall of faith. We professionals simply must attack the perilous syndromes that have captivated African-Americans of all walks of life using the invincible weapons of the gospel. We must evangelize and disciple others, pooling our individual and collective resources to accomplish the great task of spreading the gospel across all nations. Let us use our exalted professional status to do wisely, act justly, walk humbly, and witness sincerely to everyone we meet.

REFERENCES

Abbott, A. 1988. *Systems of professions.* Chicago: University of Chicago Press.

Bok, D. 1993. *The cost of talent.* New York: Free Press.

Bureau of Census. 1997. *Statistical abstract of the United States 1997.* 117th ed. Washington, D.C.: Department of Commerce, p. 410.

Frank, R. H., and P. J. Cook. 1995. *The winner-take-all society.* New York: Free Press.

Rifkin, J. 1995. *The end of work.* New York: Putnam.

OTHER TITLES FROM THE
INSTITUTE FOR BLACK FAMILY DEVELOPMENT

Men to Men

Edited by Lee N. June and Matthew Parker

Learn what it takes to succeed in all avenues of manhood, including family, faith, and vocation, from sixteen African-American Christian scholars and professionals.

Dr. Lloyd Blue, Dr. Hank Allen, Dr. Lee June, and other contributors draw on the expertise and wisdom of their chosen fields to give practical, man-to-man advice on:

- How African-American males can build powerful families
- Developing and maintaining a commitment to marriage
- Restoring African-American men, families, and communities
- Risk and failure as preludes to achievement
- Avoiding the criminal justice system
- The importance of moral character

Whether you're a pastor, educator, counselor, lay leader, or simply someone concerned with how to apply your faith to turn life's hurdles into opportunities, *Men to Men* gives you proven perspectives that can spark success and growth in your own life and in the lives of others.

ISBN: 0-310-20157-8

Available at your local Christian bookstore

Women to Women

Edited by Norvella Carter and Matthew Parker

Uncover the essence of the African-American woman that has made her a pillar both in her own community and in American society at large. This companion to *Men to Men* features fifteen African-American scholars, educators, and community leaders who have overcome through conflict and struggle sustained by prayer and a zeal for life.

PERSPECTIVES OF FIFTEEN
AFRICAN-AMERICAN
CHRISTIAN WOMEN

Norvella Carter, Ph.D.
Editor
Matthew Parker
Consulting Editor

From singlehood to sisterhood to motherhood, these writers offer seasoned perspectives on:

- How to deal with "isms"—racism, classism, and sexism
- The biblical heritage of Black women
- Facing singlehood as an African-American woman
- Rearing Christian children in today's society
- Life as a pastor's wife
- Sisterhood and mentorship.

Professionals, lay leaders, mothers, and anyone who wants to probe the full potential of their culture and their womanhood will find in *Women to Women* fresh definition, affirmation, and support plus workable solutions for life's problems and challenges.

ISBN: 0-310-20145-4

Available at your local Christian bookstore

The Black Family

Edited by Lee N. June, Preface by Matthew Parker

Explore the past and present of the African-American family and discover how to ensure its future!

Sixteen black Christian leaders, including Willie Richardson, Fred Lofton, Shirley Spencer June, and Carolyn Wallace deal with the extended family, single female parenting, teenagers, male-female relationships, the role of the church, pastoral counseling, marital counseling, sexuality, money management, sexual abuse, drug abuse, and evangelizing the African-American male.

Sponsored by Dr. Matthew Parker, President of the Institute for Black Family Development, this collection serves as an example of how the Black American community can work together to help produce stable, wise, and Bible-centered African-American families.

ISBN: 0-310-45591-X

Available at your local Christian bookstore

We want to hear from you. Please send your comments about
this book to us care of the address below. Thank you.

Zondervan Publishing House
Grand Rapids, Michigan
http://www.zondervan.com

A Division of HarperCollinsPublishers